# Searching the World for the People of Africa

Kushite Calendar Year 7861

# FEELING THE SPIRIT

## CHESTER HIGGINS JR.

BANTAM BOOKS
New York   Toronto   London   Sydney   Auckland

FEELING THE SPIRIT
A Bantam Book/October 1994

Library of Congress Cataloging-in-Publication Data

Higgins, Chester.
    Feeling the spirit : searching the world for the people of
        Africa/by Chester Higgins Jr.
            p.       cm.
    Includes bibliographical references.
    ISBN 0-553-09556-0
    1. Africa—Civilization—Pictorial works. 2. African diaspora—
Pictorial works.      I. Title.
DT14.H54      1994                                        94-4474
960—dc20                                                 CIP


*Published simultaneously in the United States and Canada*

Bantam Books are published by Bantam Books, a division of
Bantam Doubleday Dell Publishing Group, Inc. Its trademark,
consisting of the words "Bantam Books" and the portrayal of
a rooster, is Registered in U.S. Patent and Trademark Office
and in other countries. Marca Registrada.
Bantam Books, 1540 Broadway, New York, New York 10036.

PRINTED IN ITALY
0   9   8   7   6   5   4   3   2   1

*Frontispiece*

Alabama, 1968. My Great-aunt Shugg Lampley.

*To the esteemed memory of His Majesty Haile Selassie I, the late Emperor of Ethiopia.*

Emperor Haile Selassie I of Ethiopia. Addis Ababa, Ethiopia, 1973.

*And to her, Betsy Kissam, a wonderful spirit, who brought new meaning to happiness and love. I love me. I love you. I love us. Thank you for being in my life.*

# Introduction

When I consider the march of African people across time and space, the myth of Osiris comes to mind.

In the most ancient Kemet—the name the first Egyptians used to identify their nation—Osiris was one of the chief deities. Worship of Osiris is thought to predate written history, and his story exists in several manifestations in the different versions of the sacred text mislabeled The Book of the Dead, which could more appropriately be called The Theban Sacred Text of Coming Forth.

Osiris was a good and strong king married to his sister Isis. Their brother Set, being jealous of his brother's power, devised a plan to kill him. Set invited Osiris to an elaborate banquet, and when the feasting was over, he brought forth a specially designed chest. Set tricked Osiris into lying down inside it and closed the lid at once. He killed Osiris and then dismembered his body and buried the fourteen pieces throughout Egypt. The grieving widow, Isis, set out to find each of the fourteen pieces. Once she had collected them all, she fell upon the flesh and the first impossible conception occurred: She took Osiris's seed, became pregnant, and produced a son named Horus.

Horus grew up to be strong, avenged his father's death, and led the resurrection of his people and the reunification of the empire.

Through centuries of dispersion African people have mostly lost sight of their former glory. Africans are the unacknowledged heirs of the ancient Egyptian civilization that spawned writing, science, mathematics, and the very first spiritual treatise, The Book of the Dead, found in Pharaonic tombs. Today we are rediscovering our history, both written and oral. *Feeling the Spirit: Searching the World for the People of Africa* is about this dispersion and connection. The book explores the TransAtlantic communities of the African Diaspora—those communities bordering the Atlantic Ocean that extend on the east from England to South Africa and on the west from Canada to Argentina.

Today African people live on the four TransAtlantic continents in many different nations. We are a diverse people. Although we are separated by geography, national boundaries, and language, we are still similar in ways that bind us one to another. In our diversity we are much alike.

For the past twenty-six years my camera has led me on a personal odyssey and has given me entry into lives I otherwise might never have been privileged to know. I have found people of African descent, whether living in the United States, the Caribbean, South America, Europe, or Africa, mostly willing and eager to exchange ideas and share their experiences. The spirit of African people worldwide has never been extinguished, and today, with our passionate self-discovery and reawakening traditions, the flame burns ever more brightly. No matter where we live, we face daily pressures and we share many of the same ambitions. Photography has been my tool to discover, confront, examine, and depict—through dispersion and connection—the existence of people of African descent.

My intent in these photographs is to capture each moment as it happens. I try to become invisible when I shoot so that my subjects will express themselves without interference. For me this means becoming one with water, so that I can slide into crevices yet continue to flow from one space to another, going around and between the moments that comprise each situation. Water becomes my agent of transmission: It comes, it visits, it moves constantly, departing as quickly as it arrives on its way to the next moment, the next discovery.

In capturing these pure moments, I search for another important element—the spirit. Unseen but ever manifesting itself, the spirit is omnipresent. I try to record the signature of the spirit with what is apparent.

The desire—the need—to photograph first came to me during my college years at Tuskegee University. Through my acquaintance with the photographer P. H. Polk, I discovered an art form that opened an avenue of creativity and provided a voice for social commentary. Under Mr. Polk's guidance I learned how to take the camera and become a hunter of images.

I found creative direction from Arthur Rothstein, Farm Security Administration photographer and director of *Look* magazine photography, who hired me to work for the magazine right before its demise in 1971. Arthur Rothstein helped me build a visual vocabulary and showed me how to use that vocabulary to blend information in context to make statements.

My third mentor was the collage painter Romare Bearden. I think I gravitated to him because his vision of African beauty and thought was the message I wanted to convey in my own work. This creative intellectual taught me how to delineate space and find ceremony in living.

My longtime friendship with Gordon Parks—distinguished photographer, author, filmmaker, and composer—has led me to understand the value of breadth in creativity and the ongoing need to sift through my thoughts.

Cornell Capa, photographer and founder of the International Center of Photography in New York City, taught me to look for the photograph behind me after I make the one in front. His maxim that the role of photography is to show things that either need changing or are to be admired helped me understand the importance of showing the images that have always driven my photography—things to be appreciated and respected.

Over ten years ago, during a major upheaval in my personal life, Cornell, sensing my loss of direction, called me into his office. "So what are you doing?" he asked abruptly. I listed a number of things including my full-time job as a staff photographer at *The New York Times* and my research on a political biography of Emperor Haile Selassie I. "No," he countered. "I mean, what are you really doing?" Because of his prodding I went back and reassessed my work from years of photographing. I realized then that my photographic vision was worldwide and that my photographs were starting to speak to me of global connections.

*Feeling the Spirit: Searching the World for the People of Africa* is my chance to share this vision of African peoples and to highlight our extraordinary and remarkable cultures and traditions, similarities and differences that deserve celebration and have been the stimulus driving my photography for the past three decades.

—Chester Higgins Jr.
Fort Greene, Brooklyn 1994

# 1

THE mountain road took me only a hundred yards from the top. I started to run to the summit, but the air was so thin at 8,000 feet that my body tired easily. I couldn't run any longer, I had to walk. Gradually the slope gave way to the summit. The strong wind and I shared this mountain in north-central Ethiopia with grazing sheep and the shepherds who watched over them. I looked out at the vast expanse of land that rises and falls, shifting from mountain to valley and valley to mountain, all the way across the Great Rift Valley, where the remains of our most ancient ancestors were found. Indeed, this is a most ancient place.

About 3.5 million years ago, in this Great Rift Valley in Kush (Ethiopia), a woman of slight frame and short stature lived her life and passed away without so much as a gravestone surviving to mark her place. Most of the world knows her as "Lucy," named by her discoverers after a Beatles song. The locals call her *Dinquinesh*, meaning "You are a wonder!" In 1974 an American paleontological team found her skeletal remains at Hadar in the Afar portion of the Great Rift Valley. Including other sites in Ethiopia, Kenya, and Tanzania, this valley has furnished the world with more of the earliest human skeletal remains than any other region in the world.

From this cradle of humanity migrations took place in all directions: south to Zimbabwe and Azania, north along the Nile River to Sudan and Egypt, and east across the Red Sea to the Arabian Peninsula, and farther across the Indian Ocean to Persia, India,

and the chain of islands to the southeast as far away as Papua New Guinea and Australia.

Later, some thirty-five centuries ago, a second great wave of people started across the vast body of the African continent. They traveled west following the sunset until they reached the border of the Atlantic Ocean. Sometime later, during the first millennium B.C.E., evidence suggests that contemporaries of the Nok culture from land around the confluence of the Niger and Benue rivers sailed out even farther across the Atlantic Ocean. Under the direction and power of the wind and ocean currents, they are thought to have visited the American continent. It is believed they contributed knowledge delineating time and pyramidal architecture to the Olmec culture in Mexico. It is hard to interpret the giant African-looking sculpture heads and numerous smaller artifacts created by the Olmec civilization around 900 B.C.E. in any way other than as evidence of African visitors.

A third great migration took place from Senegal, Mali, and the whole Sahel belt across the Sahara and past Morocco to southern Europe, specifically the Iberian Peninsula. There these Africans, together with other Muslims and the indigenous Iberians, created the flourishing Moorish civilization of the Middle Ages, which thrived well into the modern period.

The last and fourth great movement began more than five hundred years ago, but its most concentrated activity occurred during the four hundred years spanning the sixteenth to the nineteenth centuries. From the shores of West and Central Africa,

# Most Ancient Place

*"I am the child who traverseth the road of Yesterday. I am Today for untold nations and peoples. I am the One who protecteth you for millions of years."*

The Book of the Dead

millions of people were spirited away against their will in merchant ships on the Middle Passage to build a new world in the Americas.

Between the time of Dinquinesh, the earliest evidence of human habitation, and the beginning of the Kemet (Egyptian) civilization in 8000 B.C.E., the peoples of the Great Rift and Nile valleys developed elaborate systems of writing as well as a belief system based on nature. Their development reached its peak in the pyramid culture of Kemet around the fourth millennium B.C.E., some sixty centuries ago.

Early African thought and philosophy are best described as a natural theological system of belief. Africans observed and appreciated nature—its regularities as well as its uncertainties, its bounty as well as its barrenness, its mirth as well as its wrath. They recognized the duality of nature: the aspect of it that was manifest and the aspect of it that was hidden—the phenomenal world of the senses and the noumenal world of the spirits. Things grew and reproduced; some surfaces sustained weight while others did not. The earth stretched itself to the sun by day and enveloped itself in darkness by night. The people believed that for every manifest thing, the unseen cause was a natural spirit making the hidden and latent come into being.

This theory of the natural order of things began in Kush along the Great Rift Valley and was refined by the lower Nile culture of Kemet sixty centuries ago. Today a continuation of this thinking is found in the religious rites and ceremonies of the Dogon people of Mali, of the Yoruba and Akan peoples of West Africa, as well as in those of many other African peoples.

Western cultural imperialism, however, has tried to rob Africa of much of her history. Some intellectuals on the threshold of the twenty-first century fail to acknowledge Kemet as a culture of Africans that existed for thousands of years and peaked long before the conquering Assyrians arrived in Egypt in 671 B.C.E. The ancient name Kemet simply meant "home of the blacks." Millennia later Herodotus called all of Africa Ethiopia; an Ethiopian to the ancient Greeks was a man with a burned, or black, face. Whatever name is used to describe them, the people of Kemet rose to produce the world's first civilization. This culture of the Pharaohs, according to the testimony of the ancient Greeks and Romans themselves, contributed much to their civilizations.

History by its nature requires interpretation. I am reminded of a tale told to me in the 1960s by Michael Ryder, who was a visiting professor at Tuskegee University:

*One night before his son went to sleep, a father read him a story about a fight between a man and a lion. As the story goes, the man comes upon the lion in the jungle. They have a ferocious fight, and the man wins, slaying the lion with his knife.*

*The young boy expressed his bewilderment to his father about the story's outcome. The lion is bigger than the man, and he has sharp teeth and four paws armed with fierce claws. Isn't he king of the jungle? Why doesn't the lion win? The father responded by telling his son, "The lion will win when he writes his own story."*

Ethiopia, 1992.
My son and I climbed five hundred feet to the top of this eight-thousand-foot elevation in Welo Province, Ethiopia, overlooking the Great Rift Valley. The impact on us looking over the most likely birthplace of humankind was enormous.

Cairo, Egypt, 1988. Pyramids of Giza.

The first inhabitants of Egypt are thought to have settled here from
Kush, having migrated north along the Nile River from the highlands
of the Great Rift Valley. They called themselves the nation of Kemet.

Egypt, 1973. Feluccas have been the mode of transportation along the Nile River for millennia.

Luxor, Egypt, 1988. Pillars at Medinet Habu Temple.

Saqqara, Egypt, 1988. Step Pyramid.

Esna, Egypt, 1988. Temple of Khnum.

Luxor, Egypt, 1988. The Ramesseum.

Luxor, Egypt, 1988. The Colossi of Memnon.

Luxor, Egypt, 1973. Temple of Luxor.

Lalibela, Ethiopia, 1992. Church of St. George.

Lalibela, Ethiopia, 1992.
Church of the
Savior of the World.

Lalibela, Ethiopia, 1992. Church of the Savior of the World.

Lalibela, Ethiopia, 1992.
Church of Emanuel.
In the fourth century, the official state religion of Ethiopia became Christianity. Eleven churches at Lalibela were hewn out of the solid rock of the mountains in the twelfth century. Each has been separated from the rest of the mountain by a huge surrounding trench. Inside the monolithic stone I found chiseled naves and chapels large enough to accommodate thousands, as they have over centuries. Every morning before dawn I found the Lalibela churches filled with worshipers. Savior of the World is the largest of the rock-hewn churches at Lalibela. It measures 110 feet long, 77 feet wide, and 36 feet high.

Lalibela, Ethiopia, 1992. Church of Emanuel.

Lalibela, Ethiopia, 1992.
Church of Emanuel.

Lalibela, Ethiopia, 1992.
A brotherhood of
monks lives in these
cave dwellings near
the twelfth-century
rock churches.

Welo Province,
Ethiopia, 1992.
Camels are bred in the
mountains and taken to
the markets in the valleys
today, just as they have
been for millennia.

Ireli, Mali, 1993. The Dogon people hold ceremonies around this sacred mound of rocks.

Ireli, Mali, 1993. Cliff-dwelling Dogon people migrated to Mali around the fourteenth century, replacing the Tellum people.

Senegal, 1975.

A sandstorm approaches this ancient baobab tree in the Sahel. The baobab is indigenous to the African continent.

Most Ancient Place

Djenné, Mali, 1993. Grand Mosque built in the thirteenth century, destroyed in the eighteenth, and rebuilt as an exact replica in 1904.

Agadez, Niger, 1974. I came upon this woman offering her noon prayers inside the courtyard of her family compound.

Senegal, 1973. At sunset these villagers were leaving the waterfront to return to their homes in Yoff.

Villahermosa, Mexico, 1989. Olmec stone sculpture head in La Venta Museum. The presence of these incredible stone heads with African features, probably sculpted in 900 B.C.E., suggests an African presence in the Americas long before Columbus.

# 2

IT has been twelve years since my tenth visit to the island of Gorée off the coast of Senegal. During the short twenty-minute ferry ride from Dakar, I am lulled by the hum of the boat's big motor as we slide across the belly of the harbor toward Gorée, the home of my friend the painter, Souleymane Kieta.

The island commands my attention, raising conflicting feelings. My living memory knows it as the home of Souley, his wife, Khady, and daughter Raki, his brother Cheikhou, his sister Katy, his mother, and his father, now deceased. History reminds me of the presence here of the House of Slaves. For four hundred years Dutch, Portuguese, French, and English merchants each operated the slave factory, where over time some 10 million African men, women, and children were bought, held for transfer, and then methodically shipped out to the slave labor markets of South America, the Caribbean, and North America.

Every visit to this House of Slaves is a horrifying and agonizing experience. The structure stands as a horrifying physical reminder that human beings are capable of enslaving other humans. And it is agonizing to walk through the dark dungeons past the manacles and other evidence of atrocities, where the walls echo the pain of millions.

When I enter the front doorway, I am a visitor and I am thankful that I have the freedom to leave. Inside the courtyard two graceful curving staircases lead to the merchants' second-floor quarters; in between, about one hundred feet away in the back wall, is an opening to the sea. The grand staircases and the small opening behind reveal the double personality of the space where the merchants lived comfortably while the Africans were packed beneath in dungeons, where they waited before being herded out the door onto slave ships—through the Door of No Return.

When I stand in that doorway, I feel the weight of those who were brought here against their will. Once this door was alive with terror—sucking Africans out of their homes, from their families and land. The director of this House of Slaves on Gorée is a man impassioned by history and his Africanness. Joseph N'Diaye grew up in this house, and in the 1960s he petitioned Senegal's former president Léopold Senghor to help him release it from anonymity. Today Mr. N'Diaye greets visitors to the national museum that the House of Slaves has become. He is a tireless revealer of the cruelty that the walls of this house know too well. His presentation is spellbinding and his realism horrifying. He speaks of the terror in the cramped, awful dungeons where Europeans enacted unspeakable crimes against African men, women, and children, trying to strip them of their humanity. And he speaks also of African cruelty and complicity—of the small mirrors, the barrels of rum, the guns and horses that were paid to some African chiefs for the booty of wars: other African men, women, and children who were taken from parents, husbands, wives, brothers, and sisters. Slavery was an institution driven by greed and the intoxicating lure of power. Mr. N'Diaye's fiery presentation comes alive with the too-real props left from that other time. He takes my ancestors out the door and onto the slave ships bound for the Americas.

How could anyone endure the Middle Passage? For six weeks human beings were shackled in tiers in the hold of a ship with others above and below. What could it be like not being able to move out of the way when the person above or next to you urinated or defecated and the substance and stench stuck to you?

# Middle Passage

*To the perished Africans whose bones rest at the bottom of the sea and whose souls stand before us. To the spirits of the Bijago, Senufo, Bron, Igala, Kanuri, Badiaranke, Jukun, Gwari, Landuma, Nalu, Tyapi, Felupe, Akan, Balante, Bassari, Koniagi, Malinke, Chamba, Coromante, Kongo, Makua, Nupe, Fulani, Wolof, Fang, Kono, Nzima, Sefwi, Mandingo, Anyi, Susu, Bambara, Vai, Baule, Kru, Bulom, Ewe, Fante, Fon, Ga, Ibibio, Asante, Ibo, Kissi, Temne, Baga, and the Yoruba: I salute thee.*

To have no alternative but to wait your turn of release from your chains to get on deck for fresh air and a douse from a bucket of water before being returned to the cesspool below?

The estimates of the numbers of Africans sent to the Americas over four hundred years in slave ships vary from 40 million to 100 million. About 90 percent were shipped to the Caribbean and South America; only 10 percent were brought into North America. Some 15 percent of those forced to endure the Middle Passage never survived. Those who did became the foot soldiers enslaved to open up the wealth of the Americas for their new European tribal masters: the Dutch, the Spanish, the Portuguese, the French, and the English.

The first generations brought to the Americas against their will must have known an unbearable longing to return home and unending dreams of freedom. In death many believed they would be free and their souls would fly back to Africa. A few months prior to my last trip to Gorée, I saw for myself what has to be a manifestation of these hopes and dreams at the then-just-discovered seventeenth-century African burial ground in lower Manhattan. The bones here are the remains of the first generations of Africans in New Amsterdam, some enslaved and some who had managed to buy their own freedom. They make up some of the oldest evidence of African presence in New York. For six months I spent several days a week visiting this cemetery, helping to document in photographs the unearthed remains. Here I was able to see for myself a few beads that had covered wrists and waists at death and an occasional seashell—surely currency for the afterworld. But most enlightening of all was seeing arms that had been crossed at death over the chest. This signature,

found on Egyptian mummies, is called the sign of nullification and signifies the cancellation of negative forces by positive ones, ensuring safe passage into the afterworld. In death these Africans finally reconnected with their homeland.

In the House of Slaves, I, a descendant, stand trying to guess what my ancestors felt as they disappeared out the Door of No Return, never to see Africa again in their lifetimes. Here I stand, returned. But I'm on a different side of that door at a much later and different time. I want to be able to throw a life rope through the door and pull part of me back in, back to Africa. Because of this historical rupture I do not feel 100 percent African. Over five hundred years of living in the West has produced a new coating over the color and minds of African Americans. As we seek our own history and define ourselves for ourselves, we must come to terms with a new twenty-first-century identity that survived being uprooted from the African continent.

Slavery mixed up African tribal groups—deliberately isolating us from others who spoke the same language and eradicating our memories of the place in Africa that had been home. But because of this our blood has been mixed and our ethnic bonds have been spread wider. We African Americans generally do not owe particular territorial allegiances and do not have the associated ancestral jealousies that compromise much of Africa today. Our very being embodies a Pan-African nature; we are predisposed to embracing all of Africa as home.

As I leave the House of Slaves, I stop and look out over the ocean. I take a cup of seawater, offer an acknowledgment to all the ancestral lives within me, and pour a libation to our return.

Dakar, Senegal, 1972.
House of Slaves.

Dakar, Senegal, 1993.
House of Slaves.

Dakar, Senegal, 1972. Door of No Return in the House of Slaves.

Some 10 million African men, women, and children passed through the dungeons in the House of Slaves on their way to the slave labor markets of South America, the Caribbean, and North America. For four hundred years Dutch, Portuguese, French, and English merchants in turn engaged in this trade of human life. This former slave factory, one of many along the West African coast, is located on Gorée Island in the Dakar Harbor. The building is now a national museum. On my visit there, the director demonstrated, as he so often does for visitors, some of the shackles that Africans were forced to endure. The Door of No Return was the last view of Africa shackled Africans had before being herded onto ships docked outside, ready to sail the Middle Passage.

Middle Passage

South Carolina, 1990.
Outside Charleston I came upon these former slave cabins, which have been painted and fixed up. When I was growing up in Alabama, I remember seeing some drafty, bare-wood cabins in Brundidge, but those have since been destroyed. The Africans who stayed in these cabins must have been forced to work "from can to caint"—sunrise to sunset.

New York City, 1992. African Burial Ground.

The discovery in 1992 of the African burial ground in lower Manhattan shattered several misconceptions about early seventeenth-century New York City living. Many Africans helped build New Amsterdam; some were enslaved, but others were free men and women who owned property during Dutch rule and were forced off the land by the English. Standing among the bones of these seventeenth-century refugees from Africa, I felt like I was being spiritually reconnected to Africa. Discovering the skeleton with crossed arms was exhilarating. Here was the sign of nullification, the signature found on Egyptian mummies. Today among contemporary Africans worshiping in Yoruba and some other African traditional religions, it is still made when saluting a shrine during traditional ceremonies. The nullification posture signifies crossing out the negative forces by the positive to ensure safe passage.

Middle Passage

New York City, 1992. African Burial Ground.
A Yoruba priestess and a Khamite priest from New
York City perform a libation ceremony for the
ancestors on the seventeenth-century burial site
uncovered in lower Manhattan.

Coney Island, New York City, 1990. Memorial Service.

Coney Island, New York City, 1990. Presenting an offering to Yemanja at the Memorial Service.

On the last weekend of every July, hundreds of African Americans congregate on the shores of Coney Island in Brooklyn for a Memorial Service to remember and pray for the millions of African souls lost in the Atlantic Ocean during the Middle Passage. It is estimated that 15 percent of all enslaved Africans died before reaching the Americas. This ceremony is made in the name of Yemanja, the Yoruba deity of the sea. African American priests and priestesses make libations, prepare offerings, and finally carry them out into the sea to ask Yemanja to watch over the spirits of their lost ancestors.

Coney Island, New York City, 1990.
Conch blower at the Memorial Service.

Coney Island, New York City, 1990. Memorial Service.

Middle Passage

Gonaïves, Haiti, 1991. Celebration of the Oath of Bois Caiman.

Cachoeira, Brazil, 1990. The Sisterhood of the Good Death.

The official end of slavery in the Americas came first to Haiti in 1804 and last to Brazil in 1888. I was in Gonaïves, Haiti, for the 200th anniversary celebration of the Oath of Bois Caiman. The oath was made on the night of August 14, 1791, and marked the beginning of the long, bloody revolt when the enslaved Africans defeated Napoleon's army and overthrew the French slaveholders in Haiti in 1804. Africans enslaved in Brazil were the last group to attain freedom on May 13, 1888, by royal proclamation. In Cachoeira I visited the temple of the Sisterhood of the Good Death (Boa Morte) — the death of slavery. Every August the sisterhood attracts nationwide attention when it holds a three-day vigil to commemorate African freedom in Brazil. In the Pelourinho in Salvador, Bahia, I was invited to the Society for the Protection of the Destitute, a brotherhood founded during the time of African enslavement in Brazil. This organization bound together the enslaved and the freed. At the society's headquarters I saw a trunk with two locks where contributions were kept before emancipation. Yearly the trunk was opened, the money counted and applied to buying the freedom of the enslaved.

Salvador, Brazil, 1990. Society for the Protection of the Destitute.

# 3

THE first time I stood beside the Nile River, I was humbled by its magnificence. Watching that majestic river sweep past millennia-old human deposits and listening to the force of the water and breath of the air, I experienced the confluence of the mystical, the divine, and the earthly.

I had come to experience the birth of African civilization, to kneel by the banks of the river Nile and seek replenishment—a refugee from today discovering yesterday on the way to tomorrow.

For the ancients the Nile River was the source of all life. The Nile was what distinguished early Kemet (Egypt) from the rest of the Sahara. Its yearly floodings were feared for their potential for destruction and anticipated for the fertile silt that would be left behind, vital for growing crops in the desert. The powerful forces that worked this river were deified by the ancient Keme-tians (Pharaonic Egyptians) as the Nile River spirit Hapi, depicted in paintings and sculptures with male and female characteristics, perhaps to signify the aspects of creation and rebirth that came from water.

The mysticism of water is often lost in today's fast-paced, high-tech world. Water comes to us through the tap. We turn it on and off without a thought, and most of us don't even know its source.

Rain is an inconvenience. Who thinks of crops and their need for water? Rain rarely occupies our conscious thoughts except in times of flood or drought, when it can threaten our very existence.

In Suriname I lived for a week in the rainforest village of Goense with the people who call themselves the Saramakas. Village life revolves around the Suriname River. There are no roads; it is the river that links village to village. The Saramakas still chisel and burn out logs to make canoes, and although the intrusion of the outside world has robbed them of the time and the inclination to create the exquisitely carved paddles their ancestors left behind, they still fashion their paddles by hand. They guide their boats through swirling rapids with knowledge handed down from their ancestors and help from contemporary 15-horsepower outboard motors. The village has no plumbing. Throughout the day women bring their small children and cooking utensils to the river to wash them. Men and women of all ages walk out into the river to wash their bodies twice a day; the fast-moving water protects them from the piranhas that swim close by but do not attack. Having experienced the importance of the river to the village, I appreciate the overriding power of water: I understand that the water—by

# The Living Water

*Like time, the flowing water in the river approaches me; now it's in front of me and now it passes—a steady flow on a rendezvous with tomorrow.*

its presence and by its nature—has the power to call the living, the people, unto itself.

Nowhere was this more apparent to me than in the Sahara, in Agadez, Niger, at noon: 124 degrees in the shade. In the desert each day must be planned around the availability of small amounts of water, for without water, even for a short time, you could die. The need, the search, the discovery of water, and the taking of that water, all conspire to form a human ceremony necessary for living.

In Mali my two guides, Musa Koulibably and Amadou Traore, after traveling with me from Bamako to Mopti, brought me to the bank of the river Niger. A row of huge trees hugged the bank, framing the great river as it lay in its bed. We hired a boat to take us across the Niger to the small Fulani village of Sara Seli. The bowman used a pole to push the boat out away from the bank. After he pulled up his long pole, his companion at the stern abruptly took over and an outboard motor kicked in, and we were sliding across the water, heading into tomorrow.

In Soufrière, Saint Lucia, it was the healing power of water that awakened my senses. Warm, velvety, and sulfur-laced, the water bubbled out of a dormant volcano and was piped into a tiny mineral bath. The hot sun and the gentle healing water schemed in an atmosphere of solitude to free my body of tension.

Another time, long ago, when I was six years old, I stood up to my chest in the water of a giant concrete pool. I'd made the decision to become a member of the Springfield Baptist Church in New Brockton, Alabama. This was my initiation ceremony. It was summer and the water was refreshing. I looked into the clear liquid, trying to make out the spirit whose presence had brought me here. Suddenly I heard the voice of the minister beside me. As his voice tapered off, one of his hands pressed against my back to break my fall into the water and the other pushed against my chest. My body fell back, parting the water. Above me the water rushed to replace itself, sealing my body in a welcome spiritual embrace. The arms of water soothed, but then its fingers rushed into my nose, my ears, probing every part of me. And then I was pushed back into air, where I could breathe again.

Water holds so many secrets. We search its face the way we search time. We fear it and depend on it; it can deliver us or conquer us. We use it to wash our bodies, our food, our clothes, our sanctuaries; but never can we forget that it holds the power to erase us from living memory.

Senegal, 1973.
A joyous commotion erupts along the shore in late afternoon when
the fishing boats return to the villages laden with the day's catch.

Ghana, 1973 *(following page)*.
In early morning a mother and her children collect water from the
Volta River in Ghana. The ghostly treetops in the distance are the
only reminder of the plains flooded by the waters from nearby
Akosombo Dam.

Senegal, 1972. A boy treasures a find from a fishing boat.

Ghana, 1973. The Pra River near Cape Coast.

Suriname, 1992.

The Suriname River was a major route of escape for Africans running away from plantation slavery. These Africans established Maroon communities nearly four hundred years ago in the dense rain forest of what is today called Suriname in South America. Dugout canoes, some updated with small-horsepower motors, are the most efficient means of transportation through the river's rough rapids.

Alabama, 1976. Creek fishing.

Ghana, 1975. Tidal basin fishing.

Runaway Bay, Jamaica, 1987.
When the light was just breaking,
fishermen were already preparing
for their day at sea.

Saint Lucia, 1992. A fisherman sells his catch by the sea.

Senegal, 1973. Trips to the water are frequent in rural villages.

Senegal, 1973.
The focal point of village life is often the well.

New York City, 1974.

Niger, 1974.
The Niger River is the source of water for much of the desert in Niger. At Niamey this man was bathing in the river during the dry season, when the water was only inches deep.

The Living Water

Saint Lucia, 1992.
This boat was created by chiseling and burning out a
log, a skill still practiced in Saint Lucia, as it is in other
Caribbean and South American countries where rain
forests afford access to huge logs.

Senegal, 1973. Unloading nets from commercial fishing boats.

Mali, 1993.
Getting from Mopti to the Fulani village of Sara Seli in
Mali meant hiring a boat for an hour's ride across and up
the immense Niger River. Once the boat reached deep
water and the outboard motor was started, the poleman
took time to relax on the floor of the boat just outside the
canopy designed to protect passengers from the hot sun.

Senegal, 1973.

Belize, 1992.

Each year on Garifuna Day, November 19, the Garifuna people of Dangriga, Belize, reenact the daring escape in 1823 of their rebel ancestors from massacre by the government of Honduras. Boats laden with agricultural crops enter the harbor at sunrise and mark the beginning of a day of celebration and feasting that is a national holiday in Belize.

Belize, 1992.
Garifuna Day
celebration.

Brooklyn, New York, 1970. A rainy autumn night in Fort Greene Park.

Suriname, 1992 *(opposite).* This grandmother and her small grandchild collect water daily in
the village of Goense, a Saramaka Maroon community established along the Suriname River
in the rain forest of Suriname in South America. When I visited some of these Saramaka
communities in 1992, I felt as though I had entered an Africa of a few hundred years ago.

Senegal, 1973. Fishing boats return.

The Living Water

Ivory Coast, 1973.
Waiting for the rain to end.

Ghana, 1973. A father prays over his son at sunrise.

Senegal, 1973. After a day at sea.

Mali, 1993.

In the Mali desert cash crops of onions are grown on terraced land created by the Dogon people. All day long, scores of workers bring water-filled gourds from the Niger River to irrigate the desert.

# 4

AS I look out the window, my view is distorted by streaked glass. The small plane vibrates and the sound of its engines is deafening. Below me is a vast expanse of green treetops. A narrow blue band wiggles its way through the trees, the Suriname River in the rain forest of Suriname, South America. I am on my way to visit the Maroon community of Saramakas—a sanctuary established here nearly four hundred years ago by Africans running away from slavery in the colony of Dutch Guiana.

The charter four-seater lands on a short, narrow runway of rough terrain. My journey continues by boat, a long dugout canoe with a 15-horsepower motor. An impenetrable wall of thick bush lines the river, hiding the whereabouts of the Africans, descendants of those who escaped from slavery and sought refuge here two hundred miles in the interior. Boulders and violent rapids protected the runaways from the pursuing Dutch soldiers, whose boats could not navigate the treacherous passage. The Africans collected themselves into communities and reestablished the way of life taught to them by their ancestors. A people under siege, they were required to remain ever vigilant against recapture. Even today centuries of defensive habit have taught them to plant their crops miles from their villages.

Two people on the riverbank greet our boat and lead us through a small break in the forest wall to a path, worn by the footsteps

of generations, into the village of Goense. Stepping through a portal of palm leaves that is the door of purification, we come upon the Winti Praise shrine protecting the village. Moving past a second and a third shrine, I discover I have entered a time ordered by African deities.

Goense bears the marks of centuries of human habitation: neatly swept paths, homes with elaborately carved doorways, palm trees, some tiny vegetable plots. There is personal safety here from the rampant vegetative growth of the rain forest and from the creatures, many dangerous, that live in it. Of equal importance, Goense and the other Saramaka villages provide sanctuary for African culture in the Americas.

The cultural integrity of other American Maroon communities has fared less well. All that is left of Yanga in eastern Mexico is an imposing statue. Standing proudly with a machete in his hand and purpose in his bearing is the founding father Yanga himself. Time has dispersed the African population, and what was once the identity of its people has been absorbed by Hispanic culture. At the time of my visit in 1991, only a few residents of Monte Clara reflected a mixed African, Native American, and Spanish ancestry. The name Yanga had such a familiar ring to it that I searched the maps of the African continent in the atlas; not surprisingly, the name exists in the Congo Basin and Chad.

Within the present-day borders of the United States in what is

# Sanctuaries

*Solitary by nature, I'm always in search of an exterior space that encourages and frees my interior self. A sanctuary for the body is a physical place; for the mind it seems to be a cerebral address. Their commingling gives rise to wonderment.*

now Florida, few signs remain of the sanctuary that runaway Africans once sought in the forests and swamps and among Native Americans. Unmarked graves are lost to memory in this land of the Seminole invaded by the Spanish and then the English.

The African and the Seminole, believing in a natural theology and giving offerings to the earth spirit before taking from it, must have felt strong bonds in their common battle against the European invaders. Africans, finding refuge among the Seminole, intermarried; they became blood brothers and sisters. They stood as allies, fighting against the army troops set upon them. Thousands died defending their sanctuary in a forty-year period leading up to the Civil War. Captured Africans were sent back to plantations and enslaved again, and the surviving Seminole were forcibly evicted from their ancestral homelands.

The Garifuna people in Belize, Central America, preserve the collective memory of their own beginnings by celebrating Garifuna Day each year on November 19. A mixture of Carib Indians from the Lesser Antilles and Africans thought to have escaped from shipwrecked slave ships in the 1600s, the Garifuna reenact their escape from massacre during the Honduran wars of independence in 1823.

A seafaring people, the rebellious Garifuna in Honduras had constructed boats and filled them with their people and the raw materials needed to sustain themselves in a new land. Moving up the coast of Central America in search of isolated territory, they saw the river here, named it Dangriga (meaning Crystal Water), and settled at its mouth to begin a new life. On November 19, 1992, at sunrise in Dangriga on the coast of Belize, I searched the horizon of the Caribbean Sea for the rowboats I had been told would arrive laden with people, animals, plants, seeds and roots, and the flag of the Garifuna people. In the distance my eyes make out eight boats altogether. They enter the harbor under the power of oars cutting through the water. The pale early light and the luminous sky dramatize their landing and the beginning of a peaceful new life.

As the boats pour into the harbor, thousands of people cheer, drums roll, and sirens wail. Upon hearing this seaside reception from a location in a sacred temple in town, a Garifuna priest buries an offering to the African deities and to the ancestors who made the long journey over one hundred years ago. At the harbor a ceremony is followed by a parade of the boat passengers accompanied by the townspeople to the Catholic church for mass and then to the city park for daylong festivities.

Each year the Garifuna people remind themselves and the outside world who they are and how they came to create their sanctuary in Belize. Through such cultural sanctuaries I see the survival of an identity and I understand something about the persistence of the African spirit.

Senegal, 1973.

Shoes are removed before entering traditional African homes.

Sanctuaries

Mexico, 1991. A rural home in the state of Veracruz.

Ghana, 1974. Tailors take a break with a game of checkers.

Alabama, 1969. Outside the general store.

Mali, 1992. A village elder finds refuge from the heat in the meeting house for men.

Sanctuaries
109

Senegal, 1975. The old stone houses on Gorée Island were built several hundred years ago.

Alabama, 1970. The Masonic Lodge in my hometown, New Brockton.

New York, 1977.
Early-morning coffee
in a Harlem diner.

Sanctuaries
113

Ghana, 1973.
In the third-class coach of a train from Accra to Kumasi.

Ghana, 1975. Kerosene lamps at the entrance to a home outside Accra.

Ghana, 1975. Workers' quarters at a wood processing plant in Tamale.

Ethiopia, 1992. An early-morning chore in the highlands of Welo Province.

Ethiopia, 1992. Highland homes are mostly constructed from mud and straw.

Senegal, 1972. A home construction site.

Georgia, 1971. A backyard clothesline.

Senegal, 1972.
In a fishing
village.

Ghana, 1975.
A family compound
courtyard.

Ghana, 1975.
Lovers in an apartment in Accra.

Alabama, 1971. The laundromat.

New York City, 1990. A new apartment.

Nigeria, 1975. A shoe vendor.

Senegal, 1972. A cloth merchant.

Suriname, 1992.
An African shrine
in the village of Godo
in the rain forest.

Ghana, 1973. Meditating at home.

Ghana, 1975. Out the back window.

Brazil, 1990. Going into a terriero to make obligations to the African deities in Salvador.

New York City, 1977.
Strivers' Row in Harlem.

# 5

EVERYONE in the room was Brazilian except me; they spoke Portuguese and Yoruba, I was tied to English, and yet we were together. I had become acquainted with the Candomblé priest Balbino on my earlier travels to Bahia, Brazil, but tonight he was officiating at a sacrificial ceremony in a *terriero* in Manhattan and I was here through the invitation of some Brazilian friends.

The drummer kept a 6/8 beat and Balbino shook the calabash on the downbeat. The wooden African statue, dressed in green leaves and warmed by the glow of candles, took in the chants and the music that filled the room. It waited with the living for the deities—or orishas, as they are known to Yoruba worshipers—to arrive and manifest their presence among us. And then Balbino let out a shout and the calabash fell from his hands. His body lurched back and his impassioned face was bathed in sweat. He had received the orisha. I knelt in awe at the recognition that our ancestral spirit from the Africa of five hundred years ago was with us now in New York City.

Suspended in wonder and held aloft by unknown expectations, I submitted to the beat of the drum, allowing my spirit to be drawn into the orbit of the orishas with the others. Four live chickens were brought into the room for sacrifice to the deities. Blood from their necks was directed into a bowl in front of the statue and the remainder was poured over the icon of the orisha. Then the wings were cut from the bodies and placed next to the statue, giving it the appearance of having wings to fly, and the legs were positioned in front. The feathers plucked from the chickens were spread on the statue, and the blood that had been dripped over it became the bonding element that held the feathers in place.

Quickly a line formed. One by one the people prostrated themselves before the altar of the African statue and reached out for the bowl of sacrificial blood at the foot of the altar. With the bowl in their hands and a quiet prayer in their hearts, they lowered their heads and reverently took a drink. In some the drinking of the blood caused a shiver, in some it produced a stillness like deep water.

Because blood flows in all living things, it has become the supernatural connector of all life for many religions. Christians are familiar with the mystical power attributed to the blood of Jesus Christ, symbolically represented in Communion ceremonies.

I had intended to be only a respectful observer that night, but when Balbino motioned for me to join the communion line, I did so without hesitation. For the past few years I had been inquiring and reading in my search to learn about this religion of the orishas. As I prostrated myself before the statue, I reached within to quell the objections of my Protestant upbringing and called upon the African part of myself, cut off from memory, to appreciate the full dimension of this experience.

# Spirituality

*It is to the spirit we bring hearts and souls laden with uncertainty, it is from the spirit we seek the confidence to live, and it is to the spirit we bring our pain and sorrow—hoping to lighten our emotional load.*

With the taste of the blood came a sense of oneness that took me across five hundred years and the Atlantic Ocean. During that brief encounter in the New York City of the 1990s, I felt like I had somehow stepped into the spiritual footprints of my African ancestors.

When people ask what religion I am, I say I'm spiritual. I believe in the infinite spirit, the foundation of all beliefs.

Perhaps this has allowed me to be open to all forms of worship. In the past twenty years my search for the global African personality has brought me into contact with many spiritual manifestations—some I knew only by name and others I had never heard of. But the most intense spiritual experiences for me have been delving into the African religions based on a natural theology.

Forms of this worship have been fractionalized around the globe. Many enslaved Africans of the Yoruba, Fon, Akan, as well as many other Central African peoples brought the worship of their deities with them to the Americas. In the Caribbean and South America enslaved Africans were able to worship by secretly disguising their deities in the Catholic religious ceremony of their enslavers. In North America the rigid structure of the Protestant religion and a prohibition against drum playing prevented any such deception.

In the 1950s the ancient worship of the Yoruba people was reintroduced to North America—this time by immigrants from Cuba—and later Akan immigrants from Ghana brought their beliefs back into the United States. Today the worship of African deities in the Americas takes many expressions. Through syncretism it has evolved into various forms including Candomblé and Macumba in Brazil; Santeria in Puerto Rico; Lucumi, Abakua, and Santeria in Cuba; Vodou in Haiti; Shango in Trinidad; Degu in Belize; and Winti Praise in Suriname.

A few decades ago, when African American scholars began exploring their heritage, their research and fieldwork brought them into contact with many forms of this ancient worship. They found great commonality among the many practices worldwide, even in the Americas where worship had been isolated from continental influence for hundreds of years. Through the writings of these scholars and the influence of Caribbean, South American, and continental African immigrants, some African Americans in the United States are rediscovering this worship.

Perhaps vestiges of this worship never died in the unconscious minds of Africans in the Americas. We have always poured the intensity of our faith into our ceremonies, inviting the magical, the practice of call-and-response, and the yielding to the spirit into our lives. Many Western-born Africans recognize that special spirit resonating in our worship when we join together to lift our souls to a god. I believe there is a collective memory in all of us, a memory in tune with the universal flow of life.

Alabama, 1967.
A Baptist church in Bullock County.

Alabama, 1968. My Great-aunt Shugg Lampley prayed every morning and every evening.

Ghana, 1975.
Sunday mornings at sunrise along the coast near Accra, the beaches fill with worshiping
Pentecostal Christians. Some worship alone while others come as a congregation.

Ghana, 1972.

In Koforidua, worshipers ring the *gankogwi*, or double gong, during an Akan sacred ceremony at the Drobo Festival.

Ghana, 1972.
The Drobo Festival.

Gonaïves, Haiti, 1991. Vodou ceremony.

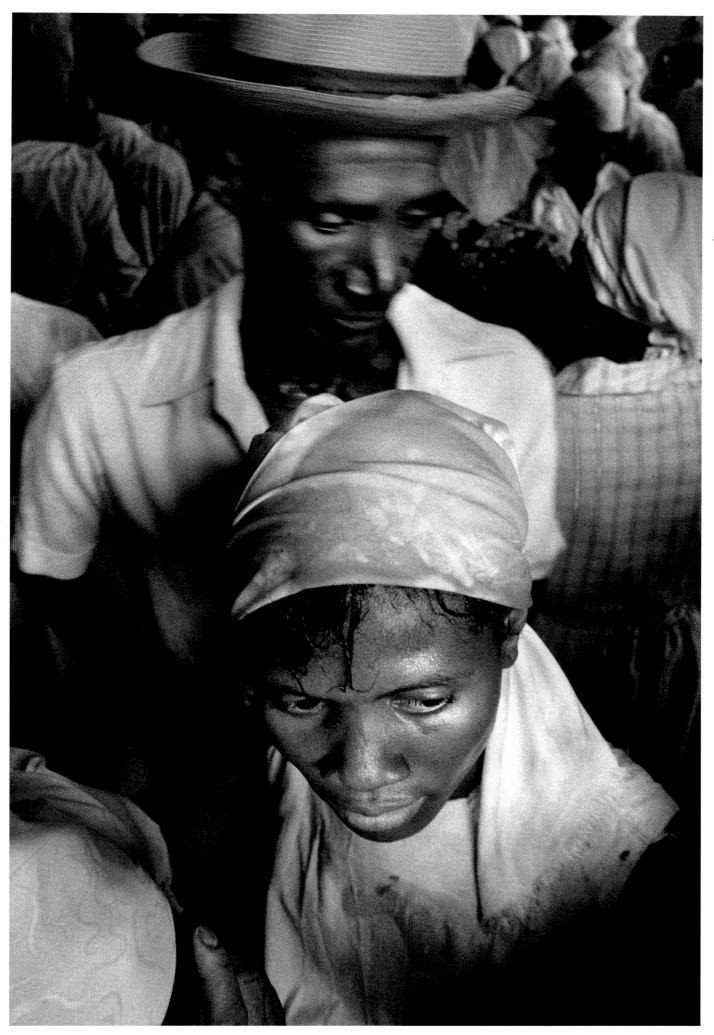

Gonaïves, Haiti, 1991. Vodou ceremony.

Haiti, 1991.
People from all the nearby towns came to
Gonaïves for Soukri Danach, a Vodou
purification ceremony.

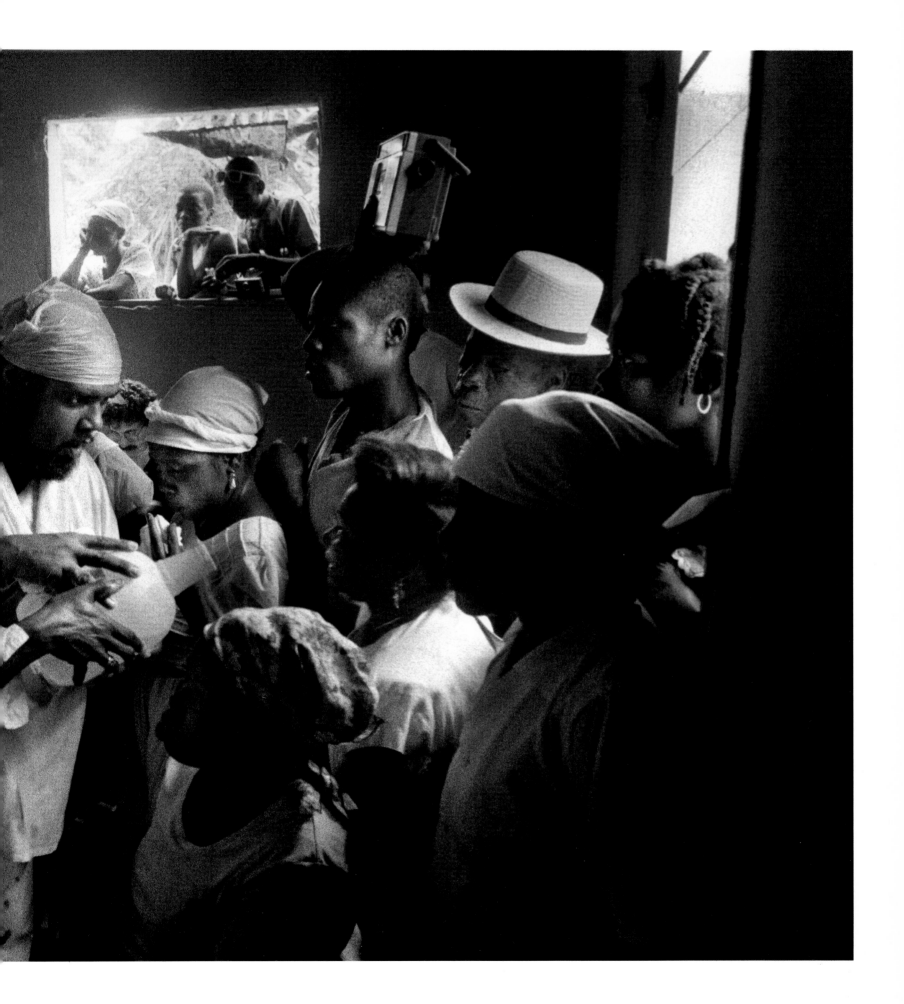

Haiti, 1991.
This woman in Port-au-Prince is walking past a cemetery mausoleum. On November 2, Haitians celebrate Fête des Morts, a day to visit cemeteries and pray for the souls of the dead.

Spirituality

Gonaïves, Haiti, 1991.
Vodou ceremony.

Matanzas, Cuba, 1993.

This Santeria ceremony took place in the evening at a private home.

Brazil, 1990 *(preceding page).*
A procession of worshipers dressed as Candomblé orishas;
it was led by Oxala, King of the Orishas, with Ogun, the
Orisha of Iron, following next on the beach outside
Salvador, Bahia. The orishas are the deities of Candomblé,
the Yoruba religion in Brazil.

Brazil, 1990.
Candomblé priestesses making offerings to Yemanja, the Yoruba
deity of the sea, during the February festival in Cachoeira, Bahia.

Tireli, Mali, 1993.
Dogon dancers perform this ceremonial Kanaga
Dance. These men dressed as woodcutters represent some of the figures of the Dogon creation
myth and show the Dogon cosmology in which the
world oscillates between chaos and order.

Tireli, Mali, 1993.
An antelope-masked figure is seen through the drummers in the Dogon ceremonial Kanaga Dance.

Senegal, 1993.
These women are using plants in a ceremony of the Ndeup healing practice in Rufisque, on the coast of Senegal. *(Following page)* The sacred vessels contain spirits from the religious ceremonies of the Ndeup practice.

New York City, 1989.

In Manhattan, Brazilian immigrants perform the Candomblé Procession of the Orishas—the Yoruba deities. *(Opposite)* Dancer Magda Silvana is dressed as Oshun, the Orisha of the River and Love.

New York City, 1990. Women with their faces painted represent purification in this Akan ancestral ceremony in Queens.

New York City, 1990. Dancing in the Akan ancestral ceremony.

New York City, 1992. The Akan ceremony making Dr. John Henrik Clarke an honorary chief of the Akan people.

New York City, 1991. Worshipers perform sacred dances at the Yoruba Shrine of Obatala in Harlem.

Spirituality

New York City, 1989. An evangelist outside Brooklyn's Prospect Park.

New York City, 1988. Inside the Ethiopian Orthodox Coptic Church in Harlem.

New York City, 1989. Immigrants from Barbados hold a mid-afternoon Spiritual Baptist service outside Prospect Park.

New York City, 1992. A sidewalk evangelist in Brooklyn.

New York, 1989. Inside a synagogue in Mount Vernon.

New York City, 1990.
In this Brooklyn mosque the room used for prayers doubles as a classroom for Koranic studies.

New York City, 1990. A young Moslem woman in Brooklyn.

New York, 1989.
After having seder with Rabbi Yhoshua Ben Yahonatan and his wife, Leana Yahonatan, I made this portrait of the couple inside their synagogue in Mount Vernon.

New York City, 1989. Commandment Keepers Synagogue.

During the high holy days in the procession of Simchat Torah, the rabbis blow the shofar, a ram's horn, while the men of the congregation carry the Torah. This procession took place in the Commandment Keepers Synagogue in Harlem. *(Opposite top)* Before Sunday services at the Holy Trinity Church, women in traditional Ethiopian *shammas* are finishing their attire with the wrapping of the *netela*. This Ethiopian Orthodox church is located in the Bronx. *(Opposite bottom)* Archbishop Yesehaq of the Holy Trinity Church reads the gospel on Holy Thursday before performing the foot-washing ceremony.

New York City, 1988. Holy Trinity Church.

New York City, 1988. Holy Trinity Church.

Spirituality

Lalibela, Ethiopia, 1993.

This Ethiopian Orthodox priest and young deacon *(opposite)*, both holding processional crosses, serve in the Lalibela churches hewn out of rock in the twelfth century.

Ethiopia, 1993.
I visited Aksum during Epiphany and was witness to this incredible sunrise procession of worshipers on their way to a nearby reservoir for a baptismal ceremony.

# 6

WE define ourselves by our manner. When I was growing up in the Deep South in the 1950s and 1960s, I became aware that African Americans identify themselves in ways that are personally distinct and yet universal.

One man in particular in my hometown of New Brockton, Alabama, epitomized for me African manner; he knew and appreciated who he was. You could always tell how David McKenzie felt by the way he dressed. His suit pants were pressed to razor sharpness, his shoes were polished to a mirror finish, and his cuff links matched his tie clip. And to top it all off, he wore a hat he called a "brim." Hats are designed to sit squarely on the head, but Mr. McKenzie always rested his forward on his head and cocked to one side. His sense of self demanded a way of expressing his personality by transforming the look. Mr. McKenzie was a man who was not afraid to be himself. I can picture him standing in a crowd or walking in the distance; you could always pick him out.

Years later, when I was in Ghana, I discovered others who were similarly tuned in to manner. Ghana, with its red-clay smell and luxuriant growth, reminded me of the Alabama of my childhood and made me feel at home. One lazy sunny afternoon I sat in the shade with Kweku Wilson and his friends—all students at the University of Ghana at Legon. Across the university quad I saw a figure walking in the distance but paid him no mind. Suddenly someone in our group asked where that Nigerian came from. Something told me Kweku's friend did not know the distant figure, and so I asked. No, he said, he didn't know him, but it

was clear he was Nigerian by his bone structure and the way he moved. I was amazed at the time; but now, after many years of observation, I too am able to make reasonable assessments of African ethnicity.

Every time I visit Africa I look forward to seeing men and women standing tall and regal in traditional African garments. The long, flowing robes impart nobility to all who wear them. On the African continent I find the embodiment of the manner I first discovered in my youth. Ironically, it seems that many continental African men and some women are giving up their traditional garments for Western dress at a time when more and more African Americans are reinforcing and celebrating their African heritage, even adopting that same traditional dress.

When I visited the Caribbean, Central and South America, and Europe, my experiences in these cultures further heightened my awareness of connections among all Africans—continental and diasporan. The concept of the African Diaspora became real for me. Among my discoveries was the largest festival in Europe, the Notting Hill Carnival, which celebrates the heritage of London's Caribbean immigrants. During the last weekend of August the streets of London's Notting Hill community fill with a half million people who come to enjoy the parade, music, costumes, and food of the Caribbean. In Germany I was invited to attend a lecture at Hamburg's All People House in the spring of 1993. As I sat with my African German hosts for a discussion following the lecture on African history and consciousness, I suddenly felt lost in time. Here in Germany in 1993 African Germans seemed to

# In Our Manner

*Rediscovering our history is the means to construct a new and total view of ourselves. With renewed discipline and vision we outlive our shortcomings. And we reemerge, having triumphed, into the first light of dawn. We are marching into a new day of our own making.*

be beginning the civil rights battle I grew up fighting in the 1960s in Alabama. This was not the first time I had encountered this feeling; talking with African Brazilians during my visit in 1990 to Bahia left me with the same sense.

African people worldwide have much to learn from each other. While we in the West suffered slavery, those who remained in Africa were forced to endure colonial dispossession. Today, as we rediscover our own histories, more and more opportunities for understanding and collaboration present themselves. In Africa in the 1990s many of the West Africans I met were exploring, at least in their minds, the possibility of economic, political, or philosophical partnerships between continental Africans and Western-born Africans living in the United States. On my last trip to Dakar, Senegal, I spent an afternoon with Mustapha Dieng, editor of *Sopi* (translating in English to Change), a progressive newspaper in that city. Actively involved in the politics of his country, Mustapha was intent on forging partnerships between Africans and African Americans to set up import-export operations and finance new businesses in Africa. He feels Africans and African Americans both have much to gain from such interactions. Of his encounters with African American tourists, he told me: "Some are stiff, some warm, some cold, some curious, and some cultivate an attitude of superiority with disdain for me—considering me part of the slave dealing—but once we interact and begin addressing our mutual needs, we discover we have much in common and that only we are capable of creating bridges to unite our communities.

"We in Africa need the help of African Americans. We need the African American lobby to work for us just as the Jewish American lobby has worked for Israel. We need changes in your immigration and foreign-aid laws. We need skilled African Americans to join us and establish commercial enterprises that will develop Africa. If every African American could save one dollar during Kwanzaa and donate it to the African Development Bank (Washington, D.C. and Abidjan, Ivory Coast), this bank could guarantee development loans for capital to enhance our infrastructure. We need to abolish high illiteracy by establishing schools that are free and good. We need the help of good minds and hard workers."

When I questioned Mustapha about the dismay some African Americans feel when they travel to the continent and find cities like the ones they left at home, he responded that "African people have both the modern and the traditional existing side by side. You must look at our families. Our tradition exists in the family. Like the Japanese, we are open-minded in our offices, but at home we are into tradition. At traditional events we put aside modernization; we believe in African ritual and cosmology. We may be Muslims or Christians, but we are all animist."

Mustapha understood the African American search for identity; it is only natural, he agreed, to seek out your ancestral identity in an effort to create a new community. Describing Africans, he said, "We are closer to nature and we react with our instincts. There is a supernatural feeling in our environment—it's unorganized and it's free. What we lack is method and organization. If we can discipline our nature, our genius will make us great."

Alabama, 1972. On the way to church.

In Our Manner

Ethiopia, 1992.
Highlanders.

Suriname, 1992. A prize catch from the rain forest.

New York City, 1975. A birthday rose.

Ghana, 1974. A fruit vendor.

Alabama, 1969. A farmer rests on his front porch.

Senegal, 1975. A woman in Dakar, the fashion capital of Africa.

Ghana, 1974. A vendor who sells to passengers on the commuter trains.

Saint Lucia, 1992.
A storyteller dedicated
to the preservation of
the cultural history of
Saint Lucia.

New York City, 1992. An African boutique in Brooklyn.

Ethiopia, 1970. A young woman in Addis Ababa.

Martinique, 1992.
Carnaval in
Fort de France.

Haiti, 1991. A Haitian vendor.

Alabama, 1968. Friends.

New York City, 1989. A Brooklyn woman.

Cuba, 1993. A street scene in Matanzas.

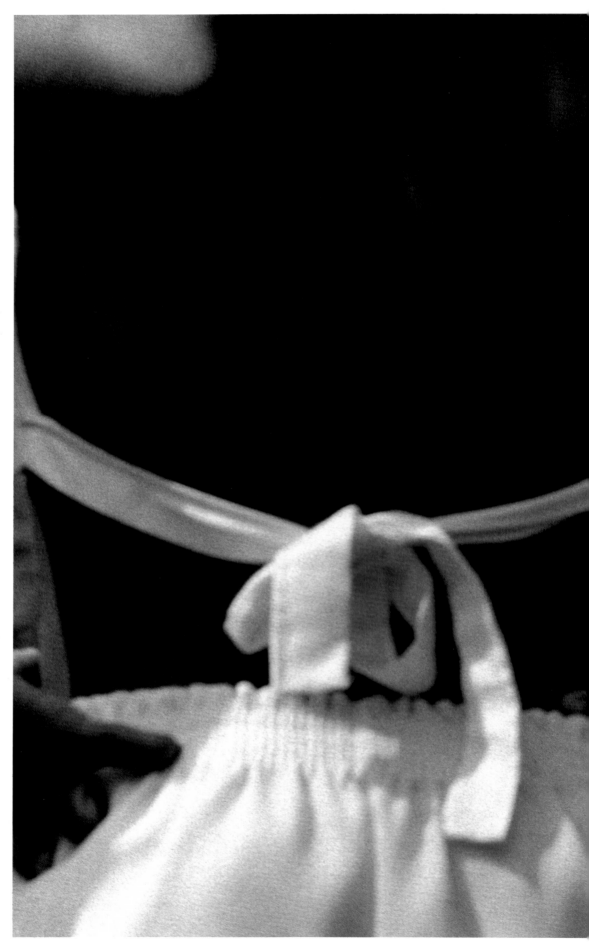

New York City, 1978.
The Confrontation.

Alabama, 1967. A front porch in Macon County.

Ethiopia, 1992. In the highlands of Welo Province.

In Our Manner

Nigeria, 1974. The hat.

Alabama, 1969. Finger snapping.

New York City, 1975.
On the East River Drive
in upper Manhattan.

Ghana, 1975. An Akan chief.

In Our Manner

Alabama, 1969.

Tree climbing.

Alabama, 1992.
My Great-uncle
Forth McGowan
is a Mason in my
hometown, New
Brockton.

In Our Manner
221

Mexico, 1991. On the front steps in Monte Clara.

Georgia, 1973. Waiting for the next customer.

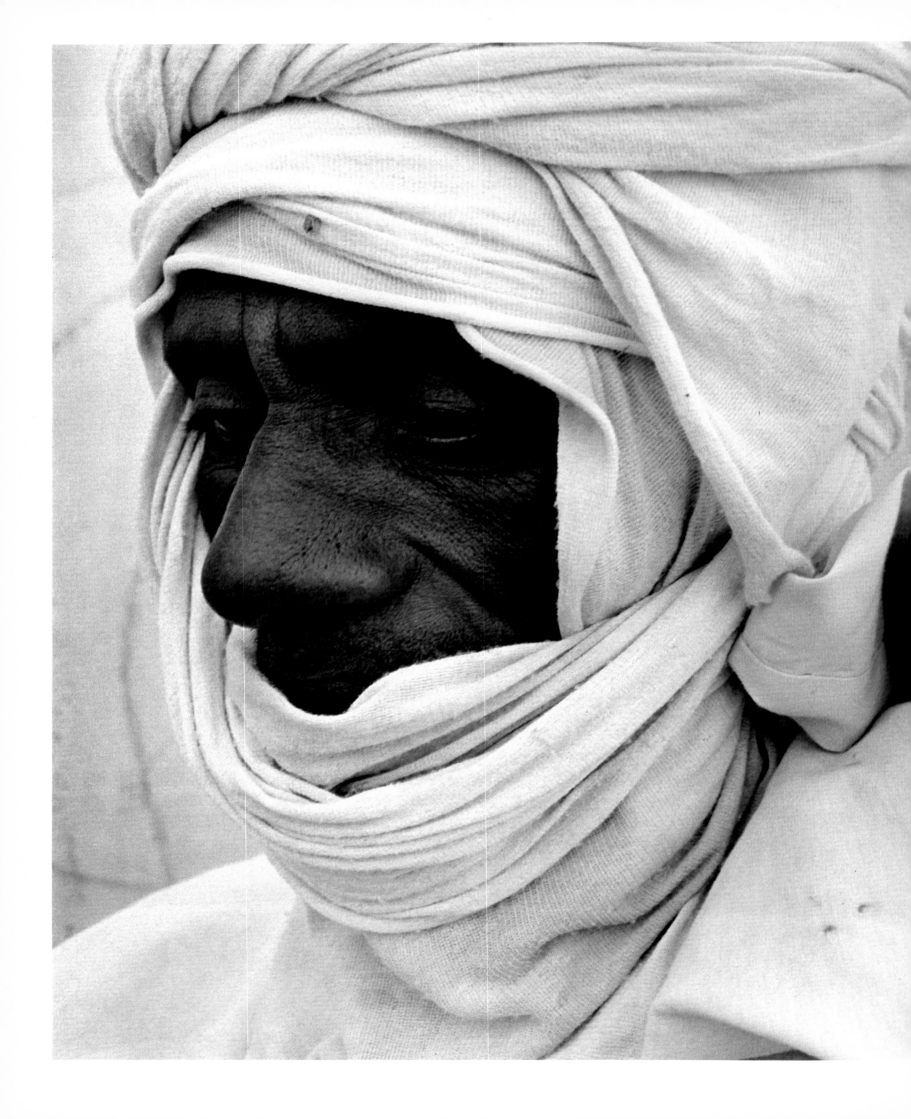

Mali, 1993.
In the Sahara Desert.

Ghana, 1975. Cowrie shells in Kumasi.

New York City, 1984. A woman in Manhattan.

Ghana, 1975. A schoolgirl in Tamale.

Cuba, 1993. At a resort in Varadero.

New York City, 1989. This woman's cheekbones reflect her Native American ancestry.

Ethiopia, 1992. A grandmother in the highlands.

# 7

I took my son Damani to Africa for the first time when he was twenty. For three weeks we explored together the past and present of our people in Egypt and Ethiopia. I wanted him to see the land of his heritage; I wanted him to experience the intense ecstasy I felt on my first African visit when I too was in my twenties.

I asked my son to come along as my assistant to help photograph the planned reinterment of Emperor Haile Selassie I on what would have been His Majesty's 100th birthday on July 23, 1992. Twenty years before, I had photographed this most amazing ruler in his capital city of Addis Ababa. The memory of being in his presence has remained an inspiration in my personal life. Damani, who has locked his hair, shares my love of His Majesty and reggae, the music of the Rastafarians who worship Selassie. I decided to add a stopover in Egypt to our itinerary so that my son could also see the pyramids, temples, and tombs of our ancestors. Because my family has no memory from which ethnic group in Africa we are descended, I decided to reach back to the beginnings of all Africans.

About two weeks before we were to travel, the reinterment of Emperor Haile Selassie was postponed. We were both deeply disappointed, but neither of us considered canceling our trip, nor did the many thousands of Rastafarians who annually gather for Emperor Selassie's birthday. While we were in the highlands of Welo Province in Ethiopia, Damani in his locks blended into the population; his enthusiasm for this ancient African country warmed my heart. On a four-day trip to visit the sacred city of Lalibela, where in the twelfth century numerous churches were hewn out of the surrounding mountains, I had a dream. In my dream I saw two men, one older and one younger, facing each other against a background of ancient temples and pyramids.

The father was speaking as he anointed the head of his son.

I became enamored with the possibility of enacting a ceremony with Damani in Africa. For the next six days I kept my ideas to myself, wondering what words to use in such a ceremony. By the time we arrived in Cairo, I was ready. I told him I wanted to perform a ceremony with him in the tombs at Luxor, Egypt. His eyes shone with unexpected anticipation. But I wondered if he would still be receptive after my next statement. I remembered that in the dream the son, although appearing to be anointed, had remained dry. I took this to mean a powder rather than water was poured on his head, but what powder? I discounted ground herbs and flowers and finally settled on sand—naturally abundant in the Sahara. Sand represents and is the land; it also contains the remains of the people. That made metaphysical sense to me; but in the real world young adults, or almost anybody for that matter, are disinclined to have sand poured in their hair.

"I will need sand to anoint your head," I told my son.

"Sand?" he asked reluctantly. "How much?"

"Just a little; you can collect some in a film canister," I added hastily. We both knew a 35 mm film canister wouldn't hold much sand. "Take the canister and find sand you feel special about, and I'll use that."

In control of the amount of sand and where it would come from, he decided to take some from the desert in the shadow of the pyramids at Giza. Days later, when we reached Luxor, he collected more from around the remains of the Temple of Karnak—one of the largest and oldest stone temples in the world.

The next afternoon we sailed across the Nile River to Thebes and to the Valley of the Kings, a basin formed by towering mountains. From the heavenly perch of the ancient Egyptian deities, the valley resembles a huge bowl to which there is one narrow

# Rites

*We are Africans not because we are born in Africa, but because Africa is born in us. Look around you and behold us in our greatness. Greatness is an African possibility; you can make it yours.*

entrance, flanked by more tall peaks. The tombs of the Pharaohs are hewn into the lower part of the mountains that form the basin. Inside each tomb twelve-foot-square passageways lead down several thousand feet into the solid rock. The scene that greets modern-day visitors to these sacred chambers is astonishing. Ornately painted walls reveal images of animals, people, and scenes that were part of the real and imaginary lives of Pharaonic Egyptians. It was here, inside one of the tombs of an Eighteenth Dynasty Pharaoh, that I chose to perform the ceremony revealed to me in my dream in Ethiopia.

In front of an enormous wall painting of Osiris, the god of resurrection, my son and I faced each other. I poured the sand he had collected into the palm of my left hand, and with my right I anointed the top of his head with this sand. Looking into his eyes, I said:

"I, your father, anoint the crown of your head with the soil of Africa. This piece of earth is a symbol of the lives of your ancestors. It is a bonding of their lives to yours. Like your father, you too are African. We are Africans not because we are born in Africa, but because Africa is born in us. Look around you and behold us in our greatness. Greatness is an African possibility; you can make it yours. Just as the great ones before you have by their deeds placed their names on history, so can you by your deeds place your name on tomorrow. You now have the rest of your life to benefit from this new awareness.

"Try your best to make your mark on life, or else you could very well die undeclared. The time will come when death will claim us all. For those of us in the Diaspora, our bodies will remain where we plant them but our souls will fly back to Africa. So here, in the company of those great ones who have waited patiently for your visit, you are loved, you are encouraged. Our faces shine toward yours. Go forward; may you live long, may you prosper and have health."

We hugged each other, feeling the spirit of the moment. Leaving him alone inside the tomb to meditate, I walked back toward the light and waited for him outside on the valley floor.

One year after my son and I journeyed to our African homeland, I found myself in Alabama standing at my mother's graveside looking across her coffin at my daughter Nataki, who was cradling her fourteen-month-old daughter Shaquila in her arms. Before my mother's coffin was sealed, my daughter and son had asked to put something from themselves inside it with their grandmother. Nataki placed a picture of Shaquila, a great-granddaughter never seen by her great-grandmother. Damani took off his bow tie and laid it beside his grandmother.

We all formed a triangle across the coffin, both my children and the baby on one side, with me on the other. I wanted us to enact the African rite of continuity I had learned about while photographing at the seventeenth-century African burial ground discovered in Manhattan in 1991. The youngest baby in the family is passed among surviving family back and forth over the body to signify the renewal of life.

We took turns handing Shaquila over my mother's body.

"The first pass is for our ancestors, those who came before us."

The second time we passed the baby, I said, "This time is for those of us left behind who are living, the survivors."

The third and final pass was for the future: "Those who will come after us."

We embraced for a moment, savoring the spirit among us of our mother, grandmother, and great-grandmother, and then we walked away so that the grave could claim her body, and her soul return to Africa.

Ghana, 1975.
Preparing for
a celebration.

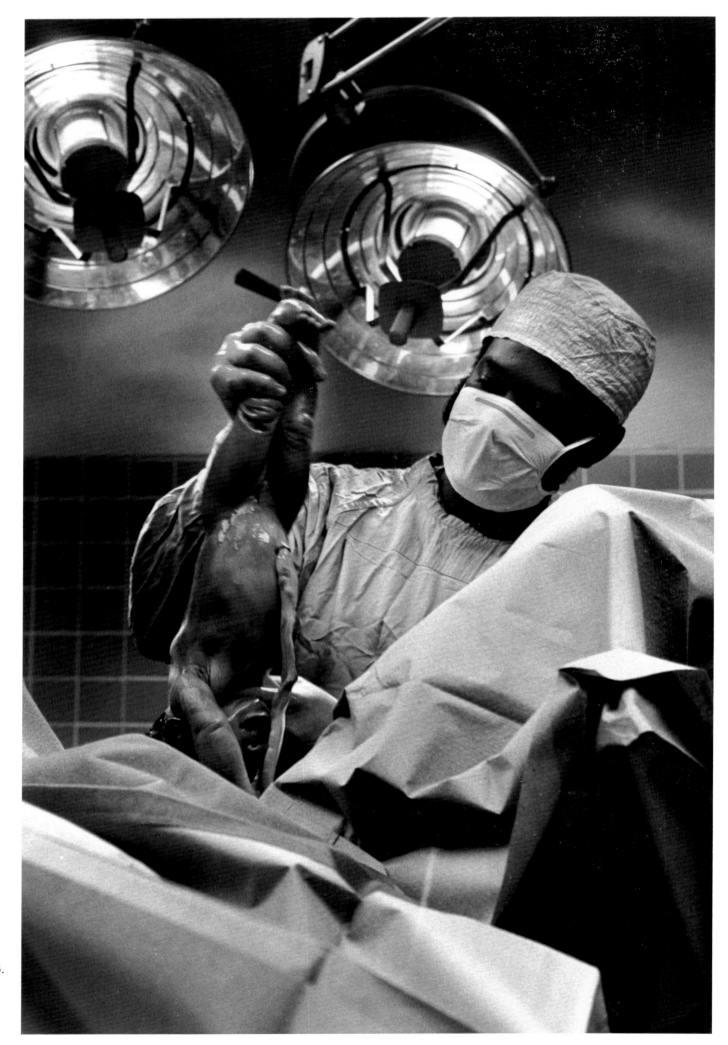

Alabama, 1973.
A university
hospital in
Tuskegee.

New York City, 1976.
Her sixth birthday.

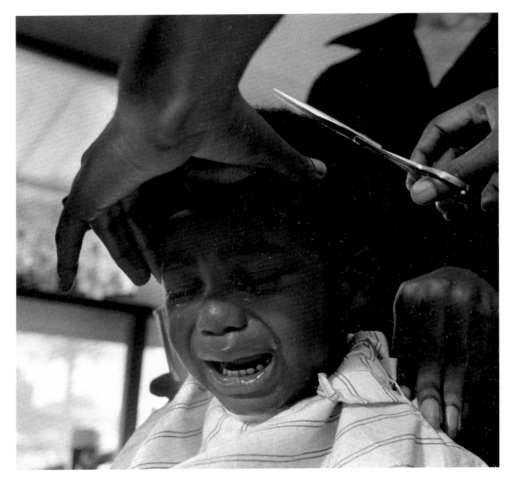

Alabama, 1969. The first haircut.

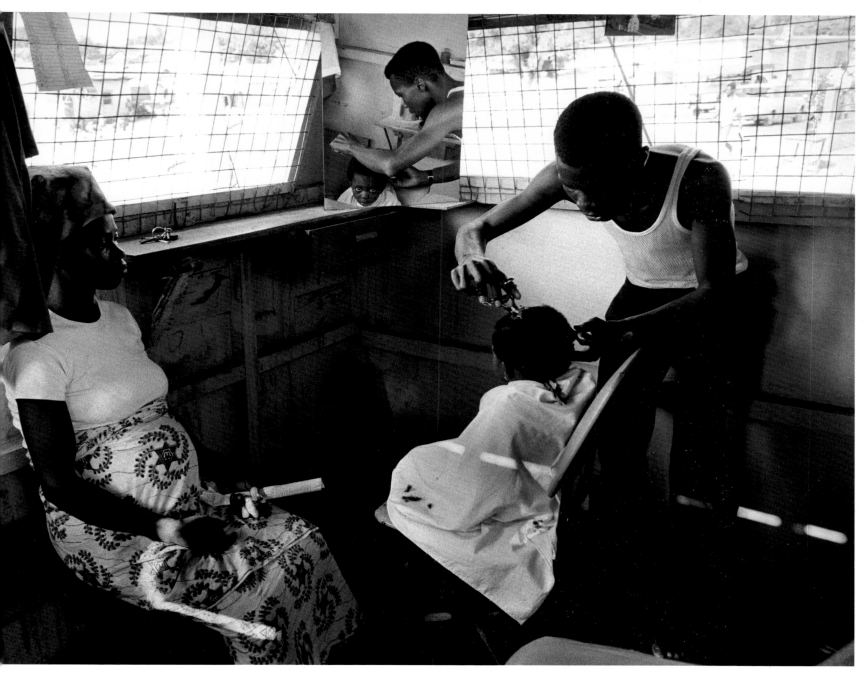

Ghana, 1973. The barbershop.

Mali, 1993.
A school in
Mopti.

Vermont, 1983. Summer camp.

New York City, 1991.
Millions turn out for the West Indian Day Parade in
Brooklyn celebrated over the Labor Day weekend.

London, England, 1993. Notting Hill Carnival.
The Notting Hill Carnival, Europe's largest street festival,
celebrates the heritage of London's Caribbean immigrants.
During the last weekend of August half a million people
come to enjoy the parade, music, costumes, and food of the
Caribbean in London's Notting Hill community. In North
America the largest celebration of Caribbean culture is the
West Indian Day Parade in Brooklyn over the Labor Day
weekend. Canada celebrates with the Toronto Caribana on
the first weekend in August.

Carriacou, Grenada, 1993.

Each year in August the people of this tiny island hold the Nation Dance, or Big Drum Ceremony. Memory of dances and drumming from the African cultures of the enslaved brought to Carriacou are kept alive through these ceremonies.

New Orleans, Louisiana, 1992. Mardi Gras.

Fort de France, Martinique, 1992. Carnaval.

Fort de France, Martinique, 1992.
Musicians play the scraper in the
Carnaval parade.

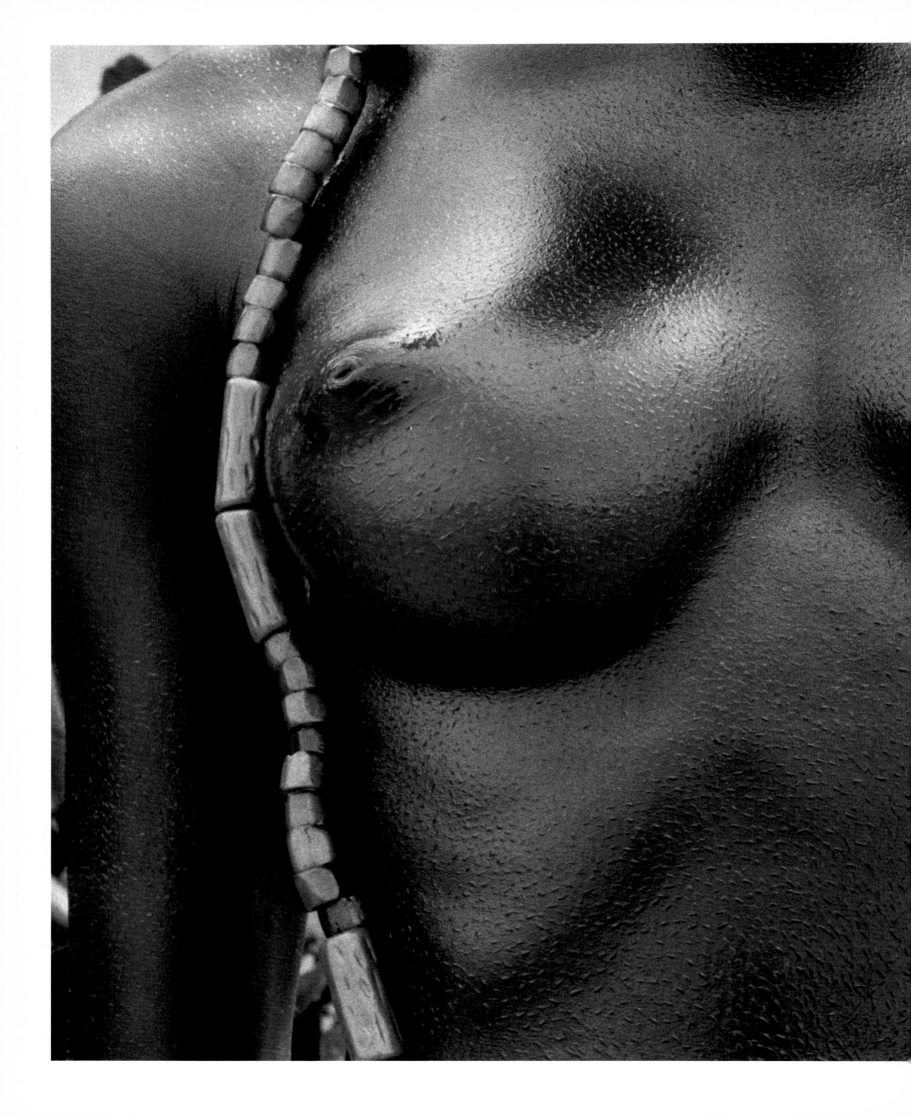

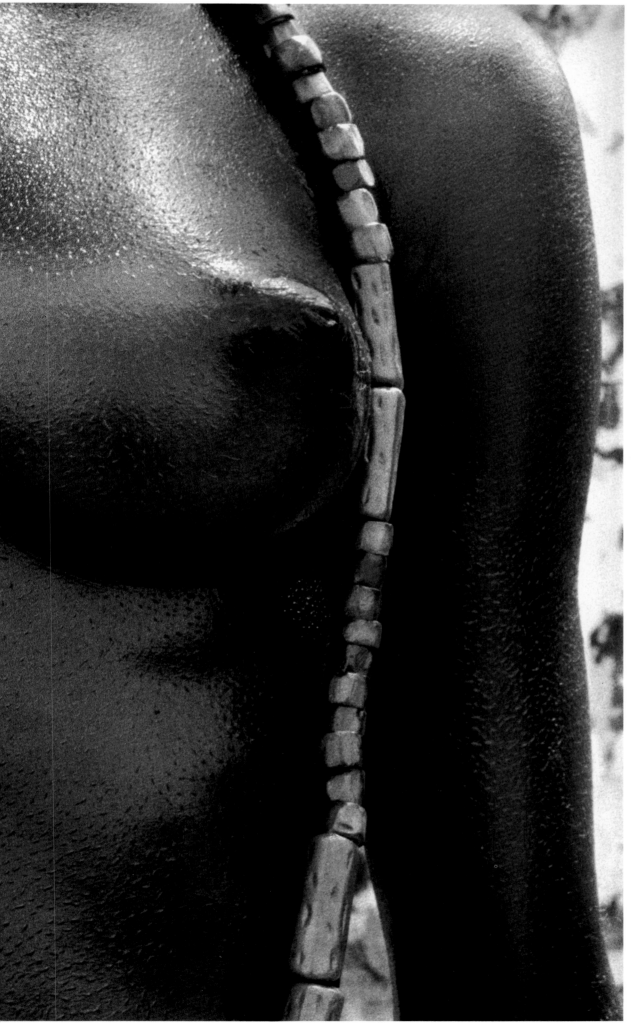

Ghana, 1975.
The parade of young virgins—a puberty rite held annually in Koforidua—takes place on the last day of the Drobo Festival.

New York City, 1990. Kwanzaa is celebrated from December 26 through January 1.

New York City, 1989. Ethiopian Hebrew wedding under the *chupa* in a Harlem synagogue.

New York City, 1992. Native Americans, some of mixed African heritage, perform the Ring Ceremony of Unity in a Queens park.

Ethiopia, 1992. The groom's party on the way to the wedding in the highlands of Ethiopia.

New York City, 1988.
Enjoying old age
in Manhattan.

Jamaica, 1981 *(preceding page).*
When Bob Marley, the prophet of Rastafari, died of brain cancer, his funeral became a national event in Jamaica. Hundreds of thousands turned out to witness his final journey. At his tomb, musician Babatunde Olatunji played the double gong, or *gankogwi,* for the fallen African.

Alabama, 1972. Burying a friend.

Haiti, 1991.
For Haitians death is considered a liberation from earthly restrictions. Outside Gonaïves these villagers were dancing with a coffin on the last mile from the church to the cemetery.

Ethiopia, 1992. Due to a scarcity of shovels in the highlands of Welo Province, graves are often dug with poles.

Ethiopia, 1992. A grave digger.

Alabama, 1967.
My Great-uncle Forth McGowan always made a point of visiting friends and acquaintances who were bedridden and hospitalized. He often sat up at night with dying friends.

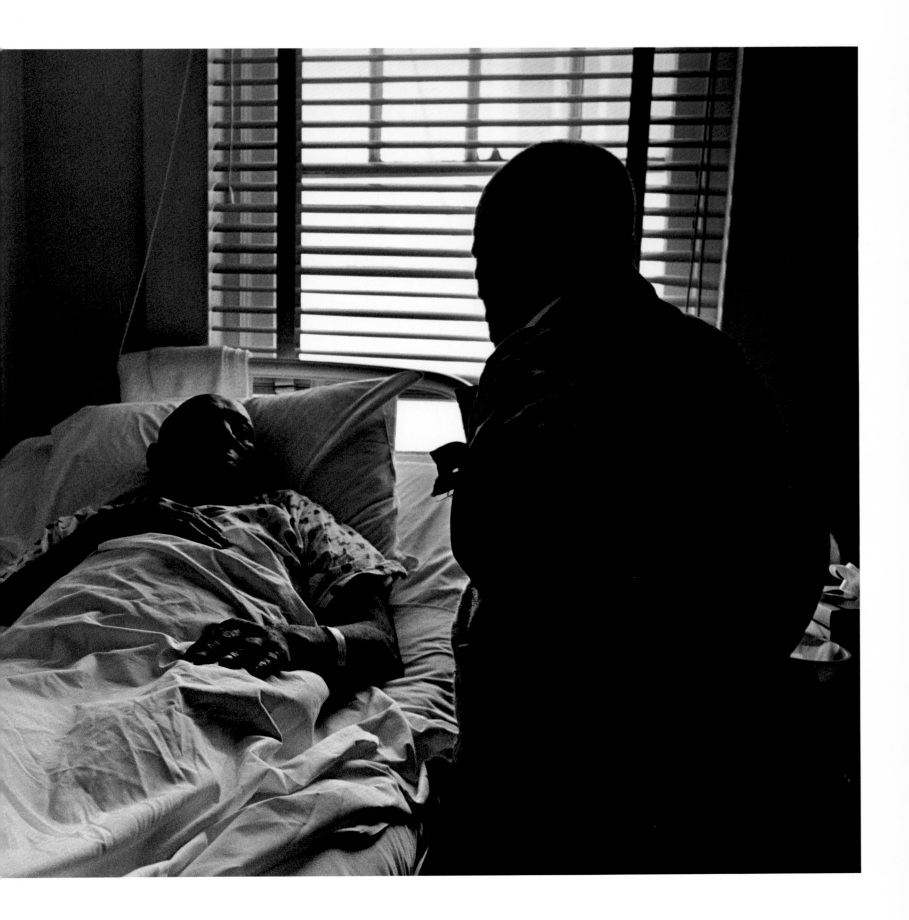

Suriname, 1992. Village elders sit with the body of the chief of Pamboko in the rain forest.

# 8

WHEN I was too young to be working, I sat some Alabama summer afternoons with my Grandmother Faith on the swing on her front porch. One such day, when the june bugs buzzed loudly overhead and zigzagged from bush to tree, we watched a seemingly endless string of wagons pass along the dirt road out front that led to the town's cotton gin. It was harvest time, and the wagons were bringing cotton bales to be sold for processing.

Loaded wagons pulled by horses rolled by, their heavy cargo making little noise. Once the wagons were unloaded, they returned past the house, this time in the opposite direction and empty of cotton bales. The empty wagons rumbled down the road, groaning at every ditch and with the looseness of the wagon parts. Grandma Faith leaned over after a particularly noisy wagon had passed. "You can always tell when a wagon is full or empty before you see it by the noise it makes," she said softly. "People's minds are the same. You take people with a lot on their minds and they tend to be quiet. It's people with very little on their minds who talk the loudest. An empty wagon makes a lot of noise."

Years later, as a young man, I arrived home from college one warm August evening to visit my Great-uncle Forth. As he was going out to his several-acre garden to collect ears of corn for dinner, I tagged along because I loved listening to this older man talk about earlier times; he would tell a story and reflect on the meaning of human actions with the wisdom of accumulated years.

Uncle Forth, with the help of a couple of other men, had built my mother's house. He was a carpenter and a brick mason, had been a cook for the railroad and in a hotel, could care for sick farm animals, supervised the sugarcane mill, was a 33rd degree Mason and custodian of the town cemetery. In his garden, in addition to long rows of corn, he would grow peas, okra, potatoes, watermelons, butter beans, spinach, and collard greens.

As he went about filling his bucket with ripe ears of corn, I began talking about how difficult it was to choose what I wanted to study at college. Next to a cornstalk, with his hand on the ear he'd chosen to pull, he began: "Well, Chester, whatever you do, it's important that you make a mark on life"—and he pulled the ear of corn from the stalk—"or else you could very well die"—he dropped the ear of corn in the bucket and looked fully at me before finishing—"undeclared."

That thought has been with me ever since. Throughout my youth my older relatives shared many such moments of inspiration with me. I remember some; more I'm sure have been lost or perhaps are waiting in my subconscious.

When I was only eight years old, I was at my Great-aunt Shugg's home when some men rushed their friend there for first-aid treatment. Aunt Shugg was the local midwife and nurse and was often called upon to treat medical emergencies because people trusted her abilities, and the trained doctor, being miles away and unable to handle every emergency, relied on her judgment. The man brought to the house was in great pain. His leg had been badly burned less than an hour earlier. It looked bad and he moaned in agony. Aunt Shugg went right to work and cleaned the wound as he lay stretched on the bed. Then she knelt down on her knees

# In Each Moment

*It is in ordinary moments that I look for the universality of life. Sometimes we influence moments, but more often we become part of them. They can be full of compassion, combining understanding with hope, and they can be routine, comforting in their familiarity. Life's meaning is often condensed into such moments that yield understanding only when we learn to accept.*

and brought her face closer for what I thought was to get a better look. But she closed her eyes and holding her hands above the wound began to mutter so silently I couldn't hear the words. As she spoke to the wound, it became clear that the intensity of the man's pain lessened until it seemed he no longer felt any. I had never seen anything like this in my eight years of living.

After the man left, I asked Aunt Shugg what she had done to stop his pain. "I talked the pain out," she said. But how, I wanted to know. "I have to locate the spirit of the pain and establish a relationship with it and convince it to leave," she answered. There is no way to rationally explain her actions, but over the next decade I often traveled with my aunt and saw her minister to the sick and deliver babies. In her practice she held to a tradition passed to her from her mother and her mother before her.

In Amsterdam, Holland, I met Norma Tevreden, who maintains a tradition learned from her mother in Suriname. In Europe, where only 4 percent of the population is African, Norma sews traditional Surinamese dresses called *kottomisies*. She explained that these very big dresses, made from bright, colorful plaids, were designed to disguise the figures of enslaved African women in Dutch Guiana (now known as Suriname) to protect them from the lust of slaveholders and the wrath of their wives. She keeps the tradition alive in her adopted country by performing with her women's group in the national Surinamese kottomisies, and she makes dolls dressed in the traditional costume. I was invited to her home to photograph her handiwork. She showed me headties, explaining that the way these were tied conveyed messages among Africans in a code not understood by European slave masters. She modeled dresses while I made pictures and her husband watched a soccer match on television, with two young granddaughters, a mixture of Surinamese and Dutch, playing at his feet.

In the United States, where many African traditions have been lost, some are being reawakened in an Americanized form and some even created. Naming ceremonies, a tradition in many African countries, are a growing trend among young African Americans. Babies are given African names by their parents in special ceremonies with relatives and friends.

In the 1960s a new tradition was created by Dr. Maulana Karenga, a cultural nationalist who heads the Institute of Pan-African Studies in California. Modeled after traditional African harvest festivals, Kwanzaa reminds celebrants of their heritage. It is intended to connect the reality of Western-born Africans with that of continental Africans. Families use the celebration from December 26 through January 1 to make children conscious of their heritage; seven candles are lit, one a night for the seven nights, with each representing a principle of living. In this ceremony of renewal we take time from today to gather unto ourselves the valuable understanding of yesterday to give birth to a tomorrow of our own making. Although the festival is always associated with the harvest, it may more properly align itself with the beginning of the season and the sowing of seeds—for its message is one of planting the knowledge of African living and traditions in our young people's hearts and minds. *Axé.*

Ghana, 1973. Village elders.

Ethiopia, 1973. Playing the *masinko*, a one-stringed fiddle, in a restaurant in the highlands of Ethiopia.

The Netherlands, 1993.

A Surinamese woman keeps alive the tradition of her ancestors in her new European homeland. Here she modeled a *kottomisie* that is the traditional costume — an extra-large dress designed to disguise the bodies of enslaved African women and discourage the lust of European slaveholders.

Cameroon, 1975.

I visited this clinic in Douala because I was told the doctors and nurses provided excellent care. As I passed through the hallways, I saw this woman in the infirmary ministering to her sick husband.

Haiti, 1991.
A small business in Port-au-Prince.

In Each Moment

Ivory Coast, 1975.
An art class in Abidjan.

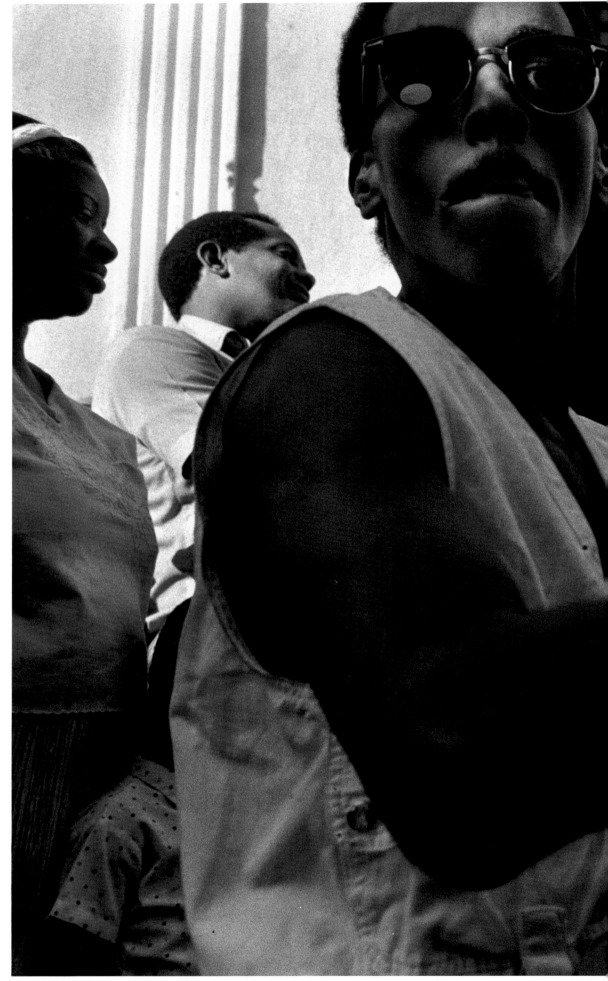

Cuba, 1993.
Musicians performing on a street in Matanzas. Of the two standing musicians, one is playing the *ekwe*, or log drum, and the other is making music with a car brake rim.

Ghana, 1973.
This man is weaving narrow strips of kente cloth
in a factory in Tamale.

Ethiopia, 1992. Weaving broadcloth in the province of Tigray.

Senegal, 1993. Repairing fishing nets in Joal-Fadiout on the Atlantic coast.

New York City, 1973.
Jazz musician King Curtis played the tenor
saxophone at the Apollo Theatre in Harlem.

Alabama, 1969.
One of my Great-uncle Forth McGowan's many skills is caring
for animals. Here he helps a cow that has just given birth.

In Each Moment

Alabama, 1968. A sugarcane mill in New Brockton.

France, 1993. A Senegalese vendor in the Paris flea market at the Porte de Clignancourt.

Senegal, 1993. This young Moslem man, known as a Bay Fall in the Mourid brotherhood, lives the life of a monk on Gorée Island.

New York City, 1991. A man barbecuing chicken for sale to the lunchtime crowds on a street in Harlem.

Mali, 1993.
A tailor works
in Djenné.

Ghana, 1973. A serving dish.

New York City, 1991. Haitian immigrants in Brooklyn make music with instruments made from hollow plastic tubing.

Haiti, 1991. Kids make music with hollow bamboo reed instruments called *vaksin* in the Creole language of Haiti.

Matanzas, Cuba, 1993. Street musicians perform with a combination of traditional and unconventional instruments.

Brazil, 1990. Grand Master João Grande plays the *berimbau* for a performance of *capoeira*, an African Brazilian martial art.

In Each Moment

Senegal, 1993. A backyard in Rufisque.

Paris, France, 1993. African street performers dramatize the consequence of self-hate, calling for unity and an end to violence in our communities.

Alabama, 1969.
A barber in Tuskegee with heroes of his generation on the wall.

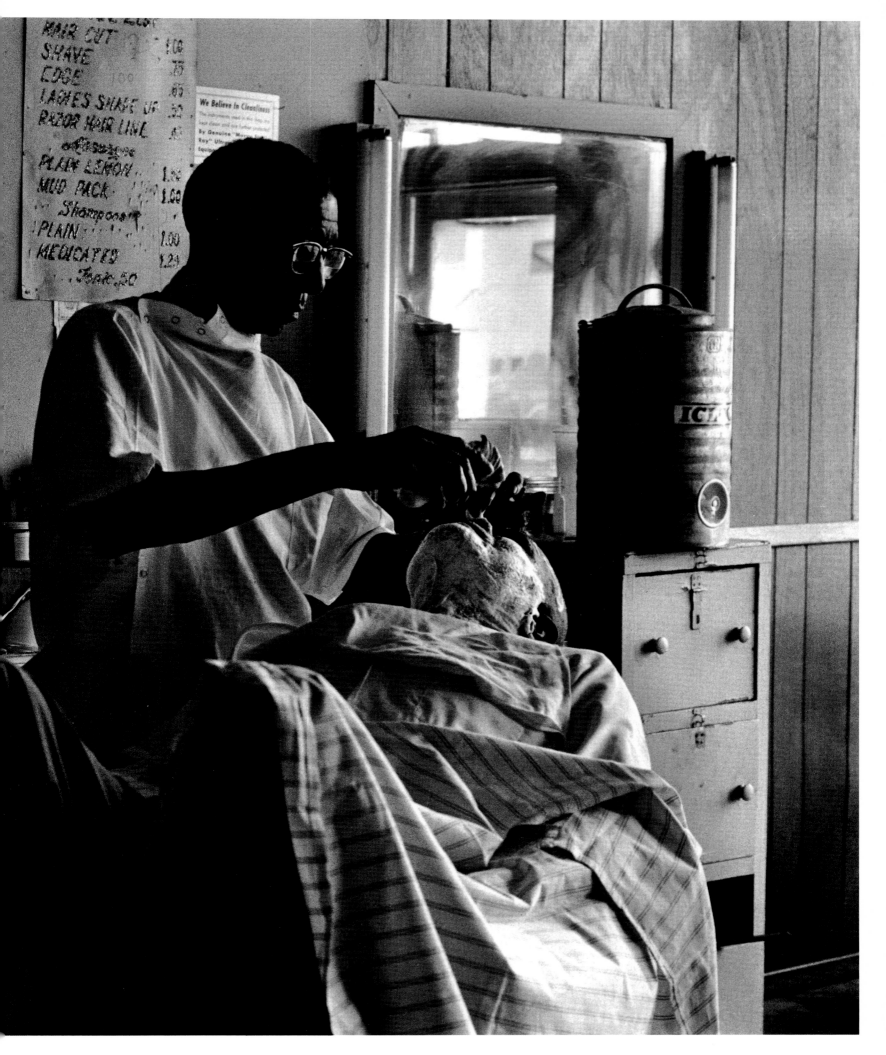

In Each Moment

Alabama, 1967. Friends.

In Each Moment

# Acknowledgments

*Feeling the Spirit: Searching the World for the People of Africa* came into being because of the millions of people who, by allowing me to witness their day-to-day living, touched me with their dignity and taught me what it means to be human.

Twenty-six years ago, when I began this project, it had no focus, no direction, and no financial support. I knew only that I wanted to correct the biased image projected onto my people by the mass media. I knew I was attempting to "eat an elephant," and there is only one way to do that: one bite at a time. Through the next three decades, with the emotional and professional support and input of friends and colleagues, I have slowly and often painfully come to grips with the breadth of this project and given it structure. It is significant that within that time the concept of the African Diaspora, born from Africanist thinking, has come to ignite imaginations worldwide.

This monumental work would not have been possible without the support of a superb production staff: Kathy Ryan, Betsy Kissam, Arnold Skolnick, Jim Pearson, Gary Schneider, and John Erdman.

Kathy Ryan, the picture editor for this project, is the award-winning photo editor of *The New York Times Magazine*. She conducts workshops and is a well-known lecturer on photography. I want to thank Kathy for serving as our quality-control engineer and for her enthusiastic and inexhaustible search through thousands of my contact sheets to discover the images that make this book. She put up with a major disruption of her daily life, living with cartons of my contacts and then images and finally Xeroxes and pasteups. The endless meetings at her loft were punctuated with the humor and helpful input of her husband, Scott Thode. I will surely miss being greeted each visit by Buster, the couple's ferociously affectionate dog.

The fine editing of writer Betsy Kissam, our structural engineer, helped me sort through the maze of words to describe this odyssey. For the past decade she has traveled with me to so many places and has become my second memory, recalling places and names with her dedication to impeccable detail.

Thanks to designer Arnold Skolnick, Chameleon Books, for his elegant book design and to Janet Froelich, whose generous spirit and artful touch made the book's cover so dynamic.

Sincerest thanks for thousands of work prints go to printer Jim Pearson, who in addition to being a master in his field is also, thankfully, a workaholic. The breadth of his knowledge of and commitment to African studies was a surprise extra.

And finally, thank you to Gary Schneider and John Erdman, whose expertise in creating the fine-toned gelatin silver prints used for reproduction took the project the last step; the quality of the final images says it all.

This work could not have been published without the timely representation of my agent, Sandra Dijkstra, and her assistant, Laura Galinson. It is due to the fine people at Bantam—Irwyn Applebaum, Don Weisberg, Lou Aronica, Janet Parker, Fran Forte, and especially my editor Rob Weisbach—that such an exhaustive work received the kind of attention it needed to come together in such a harmonious way.

Thanks to Cornell Capa, director of the International Center of Photography. At the Schomberg Center for Research into Black Culture, I want to recognize Deborah Willis Braithwaite, Miriam Jimenez, Victor Smythe, and Howard Dodson, chief curator. Extra thanks to Debbie for her constant interest in adding my African religious images from the Caribbean and South America to the Schomberg collections—selling some photographs helped defray a little of the travel costs.

Two foundations recognized the importance of this endeavor. Thanks to Bryant George at The Ford Foundation for the 1973 grant to examine in photographs the transition of a culture, sponsored by anthropologists, Drs. Elliot Skinner and Margaret Mead; and to Arch Gillies, Emily Todd, and Pamela Clapp at the Andy Warhol Foundation for a welcome 1991 grant.

To Carolyn Lee and Nancy Lee, thanks for their invaluable assistance in securing a much-needed four-month leave of absence from my daily responsibilities at *The New York Times*. Many thanks to Warren Hoge, who as editor of *The New York Times Magazine* published my extended essay on religious practices among African Americans in New York City.

To the many people who have taken time out of their own more-than-busy lives to serve as consultants and resources for this project, I am deeply indebted: Marie Brooks, Dr. John Henrik Clarke, Dr. Yvonne Daniels, Dr. Henry Louis Gates Jr., Suzanne Goldstein, Dr. Vartan Gregorian, Hailu Habtu, Dr. Ruth Simms Hamilton, Jessica Harris, Dr. Joseph E. Harris, Dr. Robert Hill, Dr. Richard Long, Dr. Abdias do Nascimento, Dr. Alvin F. Poussaint, Dr. Arnold Rampersad, Dr. Elliot Skinner, Dr. Robert Ferris Thompson, and Dr. Sheila Walker.

Thanks also to my two interns, Maluwa Myers and Gyunghwa Han, who brought organization to the clutter in my workspace.

In each country I was fortunate to meet up with fantastic guides, facilitators, and interpreters through personal contacts or seren-dipity. In Ghana: Mel Johnson, Kobina Annan, Daniel McGaffie, Atukwei Okai, Kweku Wilson, Sharon Wilkerson, Dr. Robert Lee, and Max Roach; in Senegal: John Hope Franklin Jr., Souleymane Kieta, Mustapha Dieng, Sylviane Kamara, Ousmane Sembene, and Blaise Diop; in Ethiopia: Archbishop Yesehaq, Tom John-son, Mogues Wodago, Dr. Alem Habtu, Hailu Habtu, Hanna Kebede, Gethachew Gebrhiwot, Donald Levine, Gebru Treke, Souleymane Ellison, and Victor Smythe; in Mali: Dr. Deborah L. Mack and Souleymane Coulibaly; in Nigeria: Pete Peters; in France: Gerald Noyer; in the Netherlands: Charles Jongejann and the people of Kwakoe Cultural Center in Amsterdam; in England: Margaret Busby, Ariane Braillard, Richard and Rita Pankhurst, Makeda Coaston, Nafofo Perrier, and Mesfin Yohannes; in Italy: Bruno Cattabiani; in Germany: Patrick Kan Agyemang; in Canada: Shelton Taylor; in Suriname: Nadia Ravales, Siegfried Held, Epina Majana and his wife, Beatrice, Bert Ajaiso, and Waldie Ajaiso; in Brazil: Paula Santos, Terciano Jr., Moraes Antonio Ribeiro, Pierre Verger, and Carybé; in Martinique: Xavier Orville; in Saint Lucia: Rev. Elwood St. Rose; in Haiti: Raymond Deronvil, Jackie Deronvil, Andre Pierre, Philippe Dodard, and Abujah; in Puerto Rico: Coral Caporale, Dr. Chiqui Valdez, Dr. Ricardo Alegria, Lydia Gonzales, Rafael Martinez, Enid Routie, and Dr. Vega Drued; in Carriacou: Dr. Lorna McDaniels, Christine David, and Estamene George; in Cuba: Chester King Jr.; in Belize: Pablo Lambey; and in Mexico: Dr. Gladys Casimer and Dr. Luz Maria Martinez.

All this global travel was made easier with assistance from Yveline McIntosh at Yveline's Travel; she has become a master at second-guessing me. And to my tropical disease specialist, Dr. Kevin Cahill, thanks for the ounce of prevention and the pound of cure, the few times it was needed. And thanks to my best therapeutic mirror who helped me learn to cope with the many rejections from funding sources and publishers; I am truly blessed to have Barri Novak in my life, a gift from Bert Andrews.

Last but most important, thanks to my many friends and colleagues who have always listened, always been supportive, ever willing to contribute ideas and to serve as subjects or help me find what I'm looking for. Thanks to Thelma Austin, Hugh Bell, Nana Bawuah Bonsafo, Adriane Brailland, Thomas Burke, Randall Burkett, Herchelle Challenor, Frank Cincotta, Eric Copage, Ferehywot Dagnew, Clarence Davis, Marjlijn DeJager, Leo Dillon, Ase Dinizula, Christine Douglas, Doris Edwards, Ruth Eichhorn, Obi Emekekwe, Toni Fay, Milana Frank, Natalie Frassati, Sekyere Frempong, Adriane Gaines, Michel Gelobter, Herb Gentry, Lenny Gittens, Bob Glass, Lori Grinker, Christopher Griffith, Ray Grist, Charlayne Hunter-Gault, Takae Ito, Laura James, Grace Lee, Dubaka Leigh, Lorraine Leong, Jeanette Lerman, Aminata Lo, Agnes Lorenzo, Magda Lynch, Ursula Mahoney, Claire Mangers, Tete Martinho, Bebeto Mathews, Toshi Matsushita, Lisa Merritt, Lori Merritt, Oseye Mchawi, Andrea Mohin, Zachary Morfogen, Celeste Morris, Joel Motley, Hakim Mutlaq, Kathy Phillips, Cheryl Polk, George Preston, Lynn Preston, William Price, Abdul Rahman, Chantal Reqnault, Luis Ribeiiro, Adalberto Rodriguez, Yolanda Roques, Sheila Rule, Carlos Russell, Kalamu Ya Salaam, Aracelly Santana, Hru Ankh Semahj, Carl Sharif, Moneeta Sleet, Sophia Solomon, Quincy Troupe, Mariko Uyeda, Jelon Veda, Manuel Vega, Edna Wells-Handy, Beverly Weston, Malika Whitney, Arlene Whyte, Bud Williams, Lena Williams, Terri Willliams, Mel Wright, and Angela Zubrzycki.

And to anyone inadvertently omitted, my special gratitude.

# Bibliography

Asante, Molefi Kete. *Afrocentricity.* Trenton, N.J.: Africa World Press, 1988.

*Atlas Historique de l'Afrique.* Paris: Les Editions du Jaguar, 1988.

Bernal, Martin. *Black Athena: The Afroasiatic Roots of Classical Civilization,* Vols. 1 and 2. New Brunswick, N.J.: Rutgers University Press, 1987.

The Book of the Dead. Budge, E. A. Wallis, trans. New York: Bell Publishing Company, 1960.

Budge, Sir E. A. Wallis. *A History of Ethiopia: Nubia and Abyssinia,* Vols. 1 and 2. Oosterhout, the Netherlands: Anthropological Publications, 1970 (U.S. distributor: Humanities Press, New York City).

Courlander, Harold. *The Drum and the Hoe: Life and Lore of the Haitian People.* Berkeley: University of California Press, 1960.

Crahan, Margaret E. and Franklin W. Knight, eds. *Africa and the Caribbean: The Legacies of a Link.* Baltimore, Md.: Johns Hopkins University Press, 1979.

Curtin, Philip D. *The Atlantic Slave Trade: A Census.* Madison, Wis.: University of Wisconsin Press, 1969.

Davidson, Basil. *The Search for Africa: History, Culture, Politics.* New York: Random House, 1994.

Deren, Maya. *Divine Horsemen: The Living Gods of Haiti.* Kingston, N.Y.: McPherson & Co., 1983 (reprint of 1953 edition).

*Diodorus of Sicily,* Vols. 1 through 12. Translated by C. H. Oldfather. Cambridge: Harvard University Press, 1967.

Diop, Cheikh Anta. *Precolonial Black Africa: A Comparative Study of the Political and Social Systems of Europe and Black Africa, from Antiquity to the Formation of Modern States.* Translated from the French by Harold J. Salemson. Brooklyn: Lawrence Hill Books, 1987.

Drewal, Margaret Thompson. *Yoruba Ritual: Performers, Play, Agency.* Bloomington, Ind.: Indiana University Press, 1992.

Duffy, James. *Portuguese Africa.* Cambridge: Harvard University Press, 1959.

Fagg, William. *Tribes and Forms in African Art.* New York: Tudor Publishing Co., 1965.

Fanon, Frantz. *The Wretched of the Earth.* Translated by Constance Farrington. New York: Grove Press, 1963.

Finn, Julio. *Voices of Négritude.* London: Quartet Books, 1988.

Fraginals, Manuel Moreno, ed. *Africa in Latin America: Essays on History, Culture, and Socialization.* Translated by Leonor Blum. New York: Holmes & Meier Publishers, 1984.

Gonzáles-Wippler, Migene. *The Santería Experience.* Bronx: Original Publications, 1982.

Gonzáles-Wippler, Migene. *Santería: The Religion, A Legacy of Faith, Rites and Magic.* New York: Harmony Books, 1989.

*Grand Atlas du Continent Africain.* Paris: Editions Jeune Afrique, 1973.

Holy Bible, King James Version. African Heritage Edition. Nashville: Winston Publishing, 1993.

Griaule, Marcel. *Conversations with Ogotemmêli: An Introduction to Dogon Religious Ideas.* London: Oxford University Press, 1970.

Herodotus, *Histories.* Translated by Aubrey de Selincourt. Harmondsworth: Penguin Books, 1954.

Jahn, Janheinz. *Muntu: An Outline of the New African Culture.* Translated by Marjorie Grene. New York: Grove Press, 1961.

Johanson, Donald and Maitland Edey. *Lucy: The Beginnings of Humankind.* New York: Touchstone, Simon & Schuster, 1990.

Kennedy, Ellen Conroy, ed. *The Negritude Poets: An Anthology of Translations from the French.* Foreword by Maya Angelou. New York: Thunder's Mouth Press, 1989.

Laude, Jean. *African Art of the Dogon: The Myths of the Cliff Dwellers.* New York: Viking Press, 1973.

Markovitz, Irving Leonard. *Léopold Sédar Senghor and the Politics of Negritude.* New York: Atheneum, 1969.

Massey, Gerald. *Ancient Egypt: The Light of the World,* Vols. 1 and 2. Baltimore, Md.: Black Classic Press, 1992 (first published 1907).

Murphy, Joseph M. *Working the Spirit: Ceremonies of the African Diaspora.* Boston: Beacon Press, 1994.

Nascimento, Abdias do and Elisa Larkin Nascimento. *Africans in Brazil: A Pan-African Perspective.* Trenton, N.J.: Africa World Press, 1992.

Pankhurst, Sylvia. *Ethiopia: A Cultural History.* Essex: Lalibela House, 1955.

Postma, Johannes Menne. *The Dutch in the Atlantic Slave Trade, 1600–1815.* Cambridge: Cambridge University Press, 1990.

Price, Richard and Sally. *Afro-American Arts of the Suriname Rain Forest.* Berkeley: University of California Press, 1980.

Price, Richard, ed. *Maroon Societies: Rebel Slave Communities in the Americas.* Baltimore, Md.: Johns Hopkins University Press, 1979.

Pritchard, James B., ed. *Solomon & Sheba.* London: Phaidon Press, 1974.

*The Queen of Sheba and Her Only Son Menyelek I.* Budge, Sir E. A. Wallis, trans. London: African Publication Society, 1983 (reprint of 1932 edition).

Quinn, Charlotte A. *Mandingo Kingdoms of the Senegambia: Traditionalism, Islam, and European Expansion.* Evanston, Ill.: Northwestern University Press, 1972.

Sarduy, Pedro Perez and Jean Stubbs, eds. *AfroCuba: An Anthology of Cuban Writing on Race, Politics and Culture.* Melbourne: Ocean Press, 1993 (U.S. distributor: The Talman Co., New York City).

Simpson, George Eaton. *Black Religions in the New World.* New York: Columbia University Press, 1978.

Telemaque, Eleanor Wong. *Haiti Through Its Holidays.* New York: Edward W. Blyden Press, 1980.

Thompson, Robert Farris. *Flash of the Spirit: African and Afro-American Art and Philosophy.* New York: Random House, 1983.

UNESCO. *General History of Africa,* Vols. 1 through 8. Berkeley: University of California Press, 1981.

Van Sertima, Ivan. *They Came Before Columbus: The African Presence in Ancient America.* New York: Random House, 1976.

Yuscaran, Guillermo. *Conociendo a la Gente Garifuna (The Garifuna Story—Espanol-Ingles).* Tegucigalpa, Honduras: Nuevo Sol Publications, 1983.

ENGLAND • • THE NETHERLANDS

• FRANCE

VERMONT •

NEW YORK •

SOUTH CAROLINA •
GEORGIA •

ALABAMA •

LOUISIANA •

EGYPT • •

• MEXICO

CUBA • HAITI
• BELIZE
• JAMAICA

• MARTINIQUE
• SAINT LUCIA
• CARRIACOU, GRENADA
• TRINIDAD

• MALI • NIGER

• SENEGAL

SURINAME •

IVORY COAST •

• GHANA
• NIGERIA
• CAMEROON

ETHIOPIA •

BRAZIL •

# Endnote

An African man by the name of James Henry, who was enslaved and spoke with the thick tongue of the Gullah, fought in the Civil War in the Union Army and then settled in Fairhope, Alabama. His daughter, Viney Henry Clay, was seventeen at Emancipation in 1863. She became the mother of Hester Henry, who on 03 December 1921 became the mother of Varidee Loretta Young. My mother, Varidee Loretta Young Higgins Smith, a schoolteacher, who gave birth to me on 06 November 1946, died 09 March 1993. A great tree has fallen. Here I stand on this side of the grave left with only a memory. Good night, Muhdear.